GERMAN
VISUAL DICTIONARY

Published by Collins
An imprint of HarperCollins Publishers
Westerhill Road
Bishopbriggs
Glasgow G64 2QT

HarperCollins Publishers
Macken House, 39/40 Mayor Street Upper,
Dublin 1, D01 C9W8, Ireland

First Edition 2019

10 9 8 7 6

© HarperCollins Publishers 2019

ISBN 978-0-00-829033-7

Typeset by Jouve, India

Printed in India by Replika Press Pvt. Ltd.

Acknowledgements
We would like to thank those authors and
publishers who kindly gave permission for
copyright material to be used in the Collins
Corpus. We would also like to thank Times
Newspapers Ltd for providing valuable data.

A catalogue record for this book is available
from the British Library

If you would like to comment on any aspect
of this book, please contact us at the given
address or online.
E-mail dictionaries@harpercollins.co.uk
 www.facebook.com/collinsdictionary
 @collinsdict

MANAGING EDITOR
Maree Airlie

FOR THE PUBLISHER
Gerry Breslin
Gina Macleod
Kevin Robbins
Robin Scrimgeour

CONTRIBUTORS
Lauren Reid
Anna Stevenson
Silke Zimmermann

TECHNICAL SUPPORT
Claire Dimeo

MIX
Paper from
responsible sources
FSC™ C007454

www.fsc.org

CONTENTS

FISHMONGER'S | DAS FISCHGESCHÄFT

YOU MIGHT SAY...

How fresh is this fish?
Wie frisch ist dieser Fisch?

I'd like this filleted, please.
Ich hat ihn gerne filetiert.

YOU MIGHT HEAR...

Would you like this filleted?
Hätten Sie ihn gerne filetiert?

Shall I remove the bones?
Soll ich entgräten?

VOCABULARY

fishmonger der Fischhändler / die Fischhändlerin	shellfish das Schalentier	wild wild
(fish)bone die Gräte	shell die Schale	salted gesalzen
fillet das Filet	freshwater Süßwasser-	smoked geräuchert
roe der Rogen	saltwater Meereswasser-	deboned entgrätet
scales die Schuppen *fpl*	farmed gezüchtet	filleted filetiert

YOU SHOULD KNOW...

Fishmongers often serve bread rolls with fish fillings, for a quick bite to eat.

FISH

anchovy
die Sardelle

cod
der Kabeljau

eel
der Aal

83

Whether you're on holiday or staying in a German-speaking country for a slightly longer period of time, your **Collins Visual Dictionary** is designed to help you find exactly what you need, when you need it. With over a thousand clear and helpful images, you can quickly locate the vocabulary you are looking for.

The Visual Dictionary includes:

- 10 **chapters** arranged thematically, so that you can easily find what you need to suit the situation
- **1** **images** - illustrating essential items
- **2** **YOU MIGHT SAY...** - common phrases that you might want to use
- **3** **YOU MIGHT HEAR...** - common phrases that you might come across
- **4** **VOCABULARY** - common words that you might need
- **5** **YOU SHOULD KNOW...** - tips about local customs or etiquette
- an **index** to find all images quickly and easily
- essential **phrases** and **numbers** listed on the flaps for quick reference

In order to make sure that the phrases and vocabulary in the **Collins Visual Dictionary** are presented in a way that's clear and easy to understand, we have followed certain policies when translating:

1) The polite form "Sie" (you) has been used throughout the text as this is always safe to use, even if a bit formal at times, for example:

> How old are you? **Wie alt sind Sie?**

Remember that if you are addressing an older person or someone you have just met in German, you use "Sie". However, if you are speaking to a child or someone you know well, you can use "du". If you are speaking to more than one person you know well, you should use "ihr".

Once you get to know someone, they may suggest that you use "du" instead of the more formal "Sie".

> You can call me "du". **Sie können mich duzen.**

2) The grammatical gender of German nouns has been indicated using the articles "der" (masculine), "die" (feminine) and "das" (neuter).

As the article "die" is used for all plural nouns, whatever their gender, all plural translations have been marked with the gender of the singular noun, as well as the plural marker, for example:

> potatoes **die Kartoffeln** *fpl*

5

Feminine forms of nouns have been shown with the masculine form as the main translation:

> student **der Student / die Studentin**

3) The basic form of adjectives has been shown for vocabulary items, for example:

> green **grün**

Remember that if the adjective appears before the noun in German it changes depending on whether the noun it describes is masculine, feminine or neuter, and whether it is singular or plural.

> a green salad **ein grüner Salat**
> a green jacket **eine grüne Jacke**
> a green dress **ein grünes Kleid**
> green shoes **grüne Schuhe**

FREE AUDIO

We have created a free audio resource to help you learn and practise the German words for all of the images shown in this dictionary. The German words in each chapter are spoken by native speakers, giving you the opportunity to listen to each word twice and repeat it yourself. Download the audio from the website below to learn all of the vocabulary you need for communicating in German.

www.collinsdictionary.com/resources

Whether you're going to be visiting a German-speaking country, or even living there, you'll want to be able to chat with people and get to know them better. Being able to communicate effectively with acquaintances, friends, family, and colleagues is key to becoming more confident in German in a variety of everyday situations.

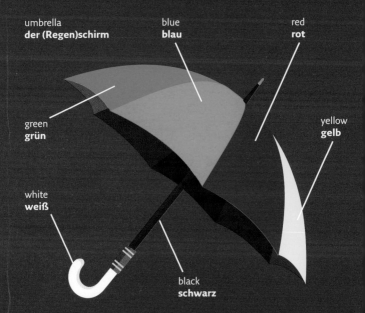

umbrella
der (Regen)schirm

blue
blau

red
rot

green
grün

yellow
gelb

white
weiß

black
schwarz

Hello.
Hallo.

Good evening.
Guten Abend.

See you on Saturday.
Bis Samstag.

Hi!
Hallo!

Goodnight.
Gute Nacht.

Bye!
Tschüss!

Good morning.
Guten Morgen.

See you soon.
Bis bald.

Have a good day/
evening!
**Schönen Tag /
Abend!**

Good afternoon.
Guten Tag.

See you tomorrow.
Bis morgen.

YOU SHOULD KNOW...

German people are quite formal when initially introduced, shaking hands upon meeting and parting. Friends and relatives will often greet each other with one kiss on the cheek. "Guten Tag" is used to greet someone during the day; "Guten Morgen" is used in the morning, and "Guten Abend" in the evening.

Yes.
Ja.

Thank you.
Vielen Dank.

I'm sorry.
Es tut mir leid.

No.
Nein.

No, thanks.
Nein, danke.

OK!
Einverstanden!

I don't know.
Ich weiß nicht.

Excuse me.
Entschuldigung.

You're welcome.
Bitte.

Please.
Bitte.

Sorry?
Wie bitte?

I don't understand.
Ich verstehe nicht.

Yes, please.
Ja, bitte.

YOU SHOULD KNOW...

"Ja" or "doch"? German has two words for "yes" – you use "ja" when answering an affirmative question, and "doch" when responding to a negative one.

When addressing a person, "Frau" and "Herr" are only used with their name, and "Frau" can refer to a married or an unmarried woman. "Fräulein" is no longer used.

How old are you?
Wie alt sind Sie?

May I ask how old you are?
Darf ich fragen, wie alt Sie sind?

When is your birthday?
Wann haben Sie Geburtstag?

I'm ... years old.
Ich bin ... (Jahre alt).

My birthday is on...
Ich habe am ... Geburtstag.

I was born in...
Ich bin ... geboren.

I'm older/younger than...
Ich bin älter / jünger als...

Where are you from?
Wo kommen Sie her?

Where do you live?
Wo wohnen Sie?

I'm from...
Ich komme aus...

... the UK.
... dem Vereinigten Königreich.

I live in...
Ich wohne in...

I'm...
Ich bin...

Scottish
schottisch

English
englisch

Irish
irisch

Welsh
walisisch

British
britisch

Are you married/single?
Sind Sie verheiratet / ledig?

I'm married.
Ich bin verheiratet.

I have a partner.
Ich habe einen Partner / eine Partnerin.

I'm single.
Ich bin ledig.

I'm divorced.
Ich bin geschieden.

I'm widowed.
Ich bin verwitwet.

Do you have any children?
Haben Sie Kinder?

I have ... children.
Ich habe ... Kinder.

I don't have any children.
Ich bin kinderlos.

YOU SHOULD KNOW...

As in the UK, it's considered impolite to ask a woman how old she is. If you must ask, use a very formal level of language – you could say "Könnte ich Sie bitten, mir zu sagen, wie alt Sie sind?" ("May I ask you to tell me how old you are?").

This is my...
Das ist mein / meine...

These are my...
Das sind meine...

husband
der Ehemann

wife
die Ehefrau

boyfriend
der Freund

girlfriend
die Freundin

partner
**der Partner /
die Partnerin**

fiancé/fiancée
**der Verlobte /
die Verlobte**

son
der Sohn

daughter
die Tochter

parents
die Eltern

father
der Vater

mother
die Mutter

brother
der Bruder

sister
die Schwester

grandfather
der Großvater

grandmother
die Großmutter

grandson
der Enkelsohn

granddaughter
die Enkelin

father-in-law
der Schwiegervater

mother-in-law
die Schwiegermutter

daughter-in-law
die Schwiegertochter

son-in-law
der Schwiegersohn

brother-in-law
der Schwager

sister-in-law
die Schwägerin

stepfather
der Stiefvater

stepmother
die Stiefmutter

stepson
der Stiefsohn

stepdaughter
die Stieftochter

uncle
der Onkel

aunt
die Tante

nephew
der Neffe

niece
die Nichte

cousin
**der Cousin /
die Cousine**

extended family
die Großfamilie

friend
**der Freund /
die Freundin**

colleague
**der Kollege /
die Kollegin**

baby
das Baby

child
das Kind

teenager
der Teenager

How are you?
Wie geht es Ihnen?

How's it going?
Wie geht's?

How is he/she?
Wie geht es ihm / ihr?

How are they?
Wie geht es ihnen?

Very well, thanks, and you?
Sehr gut, danke, und Ihnen?

Fine, thanks.
Danke, gut.

Great!
Super!

So-so.
So lala.

Not bad, thanks.
Nicht schlecht, danke.

Could be worse.
Es geht so.

I'm fine.
Mir geht es gut.

I'm tired.
Ich bin müde.

I'm hungry/thirsty.
Ich habe Hunger / Durst.

I'm full.
Ich bin satt.

I'm cold/warm.
Mir ist kalt / warm.

I am...
Ich bin...

He/She is...
Er / Sie ist...

They are...
Sie sind...

happy
glücklich

excited
aufgeregt

calm
ruhig

surprised
überrascht

annoyed
verärgert

angry
wütend

sad
traurig

worried
besorgt

afraid
verängstigt

bored
gelangweilt

I feel...
Ich fühle mich...

He/She feels...
Er / Sie fühlt sich...

They feel...
Sie fühlen sich...

well
gut

unwell
krank

better
besser

worse
schlechter

11

Where do you work?
Wo arbeiten Sie?

What do you do?
Was machen Sie beruflich?

What's your occupation?
Was ist Ihr Beruf?

Do you work/study?
Arbeiten / Studieren Sie?

I'm self-employed.
Ich bin selbstständig.

I'm unemployed.
Ich bin arbeitslos.

I'm at university.
Ich bin an der Universität.

I'm retired.
Ich bin im Ruhestand.

I'm travelling.
Ich reise.

I work from home.
Ich arbeite zu Hause.

I work part-/full-time.
Ich arbeite Teilzeit / Vollzeit.

I work as a/an...
Ich arbeite als...

I'm a/an...
Ich bin...

builder
der Maurer / die Maurerin

chef
der Koch / die Köchin

civil servant
der Beamter / die Beamtin

dentist
der Zahnarzt / die Zahnärztin

doctor
der Arzt / die Ärztin

driver
der Fahrer / die Fahrerin

electrician
der Elektriker / die Elektrikerin

engineer
der Ingenieur / die Ingenieurin

farmer
der Bauer / die Bäuerin

firefighter
der Feuerwehrmann / die Feuerwehrfrau

fisherman
der Fischer / die Fischerin

IT worker
der Informatiker / die Informatikerin

joiner
der Tischler / die Tischlerin

journalist
der Journalist / die Journalistin

lawyer
der Rechtsanwalt / die Rechtsanwältin

lecturer
der Dozent / die Dozentin

mechanic
der Mechaniker / die Mechanikerin

nurse
der Krankenpfleger / die Krankenschwester

office worker
der / die Büroangestellte

plumber
**der Klempner /
die Klempnerin**

police officer
**der Polizeibeamte /
die Polizeibeamtin**

postal worker
**der / die
Postangestellte**

sailor
**der Matrose /
die Matrosin**

salesperson
**der Verkäufer /
die Verkäuferin**

scientist
**der Wissenschaftler /
die Wissenschaftlerin**

soldier
**der Soldat /
die Soldatin**

teacher
**der Lehrer /
die Lehrerin**

vet
**der Tierarzt /
die Tierärztin**

waiter
der Kellner

waitress
die Kellnerin

I work at/in...
Ich arbeite bei...

business
das Geschäft

company
die Firma

construction site
die Baustelle

factory
die Fabrik

government
die Regierung

hospital
das Krankenhaus

hotel
das Hotel

office
das Büro

restaurant
das Restaurant

school
die Schule

shop
der Laden

When talking about somebody's occupation in German, you do not translate "a", for example "Sie ist Dozentin" meaning "She is a lecturer".

morning
der Morgen

afternoon
der Nachmittag

evening
der Abend

night
die Nacht

midday
der Mittag

midnight
die Mitternacht

What time is it?
Wie spät ist es?

It's nine o'clock.
Es ist neun Uhr.

It's ten past nine.
Es ist zehn nach neun.

It's quarter past nine.
Es ist Viertel nach neun.

It's 25 past nine.
Es ist fünf vor halb zehn.

It's half past nine.
Es ist halb zehn.

It's 20 to ten.
Es ist zwanzig vor zehn.

It's quarter to ten.
Es ist Viertel vor zehn.

It's five to ten.
Es ist fünf vor zehn.

It's 10 a.m.
Es ist zehn Uhr (morgens).

It's 5 p.m.
Es ist fünf Uhr (abends).

It's 17:30.
Es ist siebzehn Uhr dreißig.

When...?
Wann...?

... in 60 seconds/
two minutes.
... in 60 Sekunden / zwei Minuten.

... in an hour/
half an hour.
... in einer Stunde / einer halben Stunde.

... in quarter of an hour.
... in einer Viertelstunde.

today
heute

tonight
heute Abend

tomorrow
morgen

yesterday
gestern

the day after tomorrow
übermorgen

the day before
yesterday
vorgestern

early
früh

late
spät

soon
bald

later
später

now
jetzt

14

| Monday **Montag** | Wednesday **Mittwoch** | Friday **Freitag** | Sunday **Sonntag** |
| Tuesday **Dienstag** | Thursday **Donnerstag** | Saturday **Samstag** | |

January **Januar**	April **April**	July **Juli**	October **Oktober**
February **Februar**	May **Mai**	August **August**	November **November**
March **März**	June **Juni**	September **September**	December **Dezember**

day
der Tag

weekend
das Wochenende

week
die Woche

fortnight
die zwei Wochen

month
der Monat

year
das Jahr

decade
das Jahrzehnt

daily
täglich

weekly
wöchentlich

fortnightly
alle zwei Wochen

monthly
monatlich

yearly
jährlich

on Mondays
montags

every Sunday
jeden Sonntag

last/next Thursday
**am letzten /
nächsten
Donnerstag**

the week before last
die vorletzte Woche

the week after next
**die übernächste
Woche**

in February
im Februar

in 2019
in 2019

What is today's date?
**Welches Datum
haben wir heute?**

spring
der Frühling

summer
der Sommer

autumn
der Herbst

winter
der Winter

in spring/winter
im Frühling / Winter

How's the weather?
Wie ist das Wetter?

What's the forecast for today/tomorrow?
Wie ist die Wettervorhersage für heute / morgen?

How warm/cold is it?
Ist es warm / kalt?

Is it going to rain?
Wird es regnen?

What a lovely day!
So ein schöner Tag!

What awful weather!
Was für furchtbares Wetter!

It's sunny.
Es ist sonnig.

It's cloudy/misty.
Es ist bewölkt / dunstig.

It's foggy.
Es ist neblig.

It's freezing.
Es friert.

It's raining/snowing.
Es regnet / schneit.

It's windy.
Es ist windig.

It's stormy.
Es ist stürmisch.

It's changeable.
Es ist wechselhaft.

It is...
Es ist...

nice
schön

horrible
schlecht

hot
heiß

warm
warm

cool
kühl

wet
nass

humid
schwül

mild
mild

temperature
die Temperatur

sun
die Sonne

rain
der Regen

snow
der Schnee

hail
der Hagel

ice
das Eis

wind
der Wind

gale
der Sturm

mist
der Dunst

fog
der Nebel

thunder
der Donner

lightning
der Blitz

thunderstorm
das Gewitter

cloud
die Wolke

TRANSPORT | VERKEHRSMITTEL

Travelling to and around Germany has never been easier. You can travel to Germany from the UK by air, sea (via Belgium or the Netherlands), and rail (via France or Belgium – thanks to the Channel Tunnel). Germany's railway system boasts some of the fastest passenger trains in the world – it can be quicker to travel by train than by plane between certain cities – and the country is well connected by road. Local public transport is widely developed, with underground, trams, and buses.

helicopter
der Hubschrauber

rotor
der Rotor

blade
das Rotorblatt

cockpit
das Cockpit

nose
die Nase

tail
das Heck

When asking for directions, start with "Entschuldigen Sie bitte" and then simply state your destination.

YOU MIGHT SAY...

Excuse me...
Entschuldigen Sie bitte...

Where is...?
Wo ist...?

Which way is...?
Wo liegt...?

What's the quickest way to...?
Wie komme ich am schnellsten zu / nach...?

How far away is it?
Wie weit ist es?

Is it far from here?
Ist es weit?

I'm lost.
Ich habe mich verirrt.

I'm looking for...
Ich suche...

I'm going...
Ich möchte nach / zu...

Can I walk there?
Kann ich dahin zu Fuß gehen?

I'll take a taxi to the station.
Ich nehme ein Taxi zum Bahnhof.

YOU MIGHT HEAR...

It's over there.
Es ist dort drüben.

It's in the other direction.
Das liegt in der anderen Richtung.

It's ... metres/minutes from here.
Es ist ... Meter / Minuten von hier entfernt.

Go straight ahead.
Immer geradeaus.

Turn left/right.
Biegen Sie links / rechts ab.

It's next to...
Es ist neben...

It's opposite...
Es liegt gegenüber von...

It's near...
Es ist in der Nähe von...

Follow the signs for...
Gehen / Fahren Sie in Richtung...

street **die Straße**	traffic jam **der Verkehrsstau**	route **die Route**
commuter **der Pendler /** **die Pendlerin**	rush hour **die** **Hauptverkehrszeit**	to walk **gehen**
driver **der Fahrer /** **die Fahrerin**	public transport **die öffentlichen** **Verkehrsmittel** *ntpl*	to drive **fahren** to return **zurückkehren**
passenger **der Passagier /** **die Passagierin**	taxi **das Taxi**	to cross **überqueren**
pedestrian **der Fußgänger /** **die Fußgängerin**	taxi rank **der Taxistand**	to turn **abbiegen**
traffic **der Verkehr**	directions **die Anweisungen** *fpl*	to commute **pendeln**

YOU SHOULD KNOW...

At pedestrian crossings, be aware that you must stop when the light turns to amber and before it turns red.

map **die Landkarte**	ticket **die Fahrkarte**	timetable **der Zeitplan**

Traffic drives on the right-hand side in Germany – vehicles must give way to drivers approaching from their right at intersections, but from their left on roundabouts! Remember to carry your driving licence, proof of insurance, ID, and car registration documents with you while driving in Germany.

YOU MIGHT SAY...

Is this the road to...?
Ist das der Weg nach / zu...?

Can I park here?
Kann ich hier parken?

Do I have to pay to park?
Ist das Parken kostenpflichtig?

Where can I hire a car?
Wo kann ich ein Auto mieten?

I'd like to hire a car...
Ich würde gern ein Auto mieten...

... for four days/a week.
... für vier Tage / eine Woche.

What is your daily/weekly rate?
Was ist Ihr Preis pro Tag / Woche?

When/Where must I return it?
Wann / Wohin soll ich es zurückbringen?

Where is the nearest petrol station?
Wo ist die nächste Tankstelle?

I'd like ... litres of fuel, please.
... Liter Benzin, bitte.

YOU MIGHT HEAR...

You can/can't park here.
Hier können Sie parken / nicht parken.

It's free to park here.
Das Parken ist hier kostenlos.

It costs ... to park here.
Das Parken kostet hier...

Car hire is ... per day/week.
Der Mietpreis für ein Auto ist ... pro Tag / Woche.

May I see your documents, please?
Ihre Papiere, bitte.

Please return it to...
Bringen Sie es bitte nach / zu ... zurück.

Please return the car with a full tank of fuel.
Bitte bringen Sie das Auto aufgetankt zurück.

Which pump are you at?
An welcher Zapfsäule sind Sie?

How much fuel would you like?
Wie viel Benzin möchten Sie?

VOCABULARY

people carrier der Minivan	hybrid das Hybridauto	transmission das Getriebe
motorhome das Wohnmobil	engine der Motor	Breathalyser® der Promillemesser
caravan der Wohnwagen	battery die Batterie	to start the engine den Motor anlassen
passenger seat der Beifahrersitz	brake die Bremse	to brake bremsen
driver's seat der Fahrersitz	accelerator das Gaspedal	to overtake überholen
back seat der Rücksitz	air conditioning die Klimaanlage	to park parken
child seat der Kindersitz	clutch die Kupplung	to reverse zurücksetzen
roof rack der Dachgepäckträger	cruise control der Tempomat	to slow down verlangsamen
sunroof das Schiebedach	exhaust (pipe) das Auspuffrohr	to speed die Geschwindigkeit überschreiten
automatic die Automatik	fuel tank der Benzintank	to stop anhalten
electric car das Elektroauto	gearbox das Schaltgetriebe	

YOU SHOULD KNOW...

Sat navs that are able to detect speed cameras are illegal in Germany: many UK sat navs have this feature, so take care to disable this option if you wish to use your sat nav while driving in Germany.

boot
der Kofferraum

roof
das Dach

window
das Fenster

wheel
das Rad

door
die Tür

wing
der Kotflügel

tyre
der Autoreifen

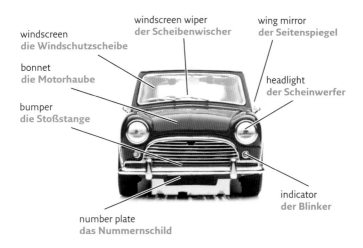

windscreen wiper
der Scheibenwischer

wing mirror
der Seitenspiegel

windscreen
die Windschutzscheibe

bonnet
die Motorhaube

headlight
der Scheinwerfer

bumper
die Stoßstange

indicator
der Blinker

number plate
das Nummernschild

dashboard
das Armaturenbrett

fuel gauge
die Tankanzeige

gear stick
der Schaltknüppel

glove compartment
das Handschuhfach

handbrake
die Handbremse

headrest
die Kopfstütze

ignition
die Zündung

rearview mirror
der Rückspiegel

sat nav
das Navi

seatbelt
der Sicherheitsgurt

speedometer
der Tachometer

steering wheel
das Lenkrad

Germany has an excellent motorway system free of charge, and there is no speed limit. Be aware, though, that there are often temporary speed restrictions which must be respected. Also, be careful when you overtake that the way is clear, as there may be another car coming up behind you at high speed. You must then swing back into the right-hand lane as soon as possible.

VOCABULARY

dual carriageway
die Schnellstraße

single-track road
die einspurige Landstraße

tarmac®
der Asphalt

corner
die Ecke

exit
die Ausfahrt

slip road
die Zufahrtsstraße

layby
die Parkbucht

speed limit
die Geschwindig-keitsbegrenzung

diversion
die Umleitung

driving licence
der Führerschein

car registration document
der Fahrzeugschein

car insurance
die Kfz-Versicherung

car hire/rental
die Autovermietung

unleaded petrol
das bleifreie Benzin

diesel
der Diesel

roadworks
die Straßenarbeiten *fpl*

YOU SHOULD KNOW...

Speed limits on German roads go by kmph, not mph. In dry weather, the limits are 50 kmph (31 mph) in built-up areas and 100 kmph (62 mph) on two-lane highways (unless otherwise indicated). There are no speed limits other than temporary ones on dual carriageways and motorways, but note that 130 kmph is the recommended top speed. In some places, there may be speed limits in wet weather ("bei Nässe").

accessible parking space
**der Behinderten-
parkplatz**

bridge
die Brücke

car park
der Parkplatz

car wash
**die
Autowaschanlage**

fuel pump
die Zapfsäule

junction
die Kreuzung

kerb
die Bordkante

lane
die Fahrspur

level crossing
der Bahnübergang

motorway
die Autobahn

parking meter
die Parkuhr

parking space
die Parklücke

pavement
der Bürgersteig

petrol station
die Tankstelle

pothole
das Schlagloch

road
die Straße

roundabout
der Kreisverkehr

service area
die Raststätte

speed camera
**die Geschwindig-
keitskamera**

traffic cone
der Pylon

traffic lights
die Verkehrsampel

traffic warden
**der Verkehrspolizist /
die Verkehrspolizistin**

tunnel
der Tunnel

zebra crossing
der Zebrastreifen

If you break down on the motorway, put on a hi-viz vest, set up the warning triangle, then call the police or the breakdown service operating in that area using one of the orange emergency telephones that are located every 2 km along the side of the road. Otherwise, call 112 to contact the emergency services.

YOU MIGHT SAY...

Can you help me?
Können Sie mir helfen?

I've broken down.
Mein Auto hat versagt.

I've had an accident.
Ich hatte einen Unfall.

I've run out of petrol.
Mir ist das Benzin ausgegangen.

I've got a flat tyre.
Ich habe einen platten Reifen.

I've lost my car keys.
Ich habe meinen Autoschlüssel verloren.

The car won't start.
Das Auto startet nicht.

There's a problem with...
Wir haben ein Problem mit...

I've been injured.
Ich bin verletzt.

Can you send a breakdown van?
Können Sie einen Abschleppwagen schicken?

Is there a garage/petrol station nearby?
Gibt es in der Nähe eine Werkstatt / eine Tankstelle?

Can you tow me to a garage?
Können Sie mich bis zur Werkstatt abschleppen?

Can you help me change this wheel?
Können Sie mir helfen, das Rad zu wechseln?

How much will a repair cost?
Wie viel kostet die Reparatur?

When will the car be fixed?
Bis wann können Sie das Auto reparieren?

May I take your insurance details?
Können Sie mir Eden Namen Ihrer Versicherung und Ihre Versicherungsnummer geben?

Do you need any help?
Kann ich Ihnen helfen?

Are you hurt?
Sind sie verletzt?

What's wrong with your car?
Was ist mit Ihrem Auto los?

Where have you broken down?
Wo ist Ihr Auto liegengeblieben?

I can tow you to...
Ich kann Sie bis ... abschleppen.

I can give you a jumpstart.
Ich kann Ihnen Starthilfe geben.

The repairs will cost...
Die Reparatur wird ... kosten.

We need to order new parts.
Wir müssen Ersatzteile bestellen.

The car will be ready by...
Das Auto wird ... fertig sein.

I need your insurance details.
Ich brauche die Kontaktdaten Ihrer Versicherung.

Call an ambulance/the police!
Rufen Sie den Rettungsdienst / die Polizei!

VOCABULARY

accident **der Unfall**	flat tyre **der platte Reifen**	to have a flat tyre **einen platten Reifen haben**
breakdown **die Panne**	to break down **kaputtgehen**	to change a tyre **den Reifen wechseln**
collision **der Zusammenstoß**	to have an accident **einen Unfall haben**	to tow **abschleppen**

YOU SHOULD KNOW...

When driving in Germany, you are legally required to have the following in your car: headlight converters; spare bulbs; warning triangles; hi-viz vests; and a Breathalyser® kit. You must also display a GB car sticker if you are driving a UK-registered vehicle.

airbag
der Airbag

antifreeze
das Frostschutzmittel

emergency phone
das Notruftelefon

garage
die Garage

hi-viz vest
die Warnweste

jack
der Wagenheber

jump leads
die Starthilfekabel *ntpl*

mechanic
der Mechaniker / die Mechanikerin

snow chains
die Schneeketten *fpl*

spare wheel
das Reserverad

tow truck
der Abschleppwagen

warning triangle
das Warndreieck

Local bus and trolleybus services are often well organized and useful; for longer journeys, rail services are usually faster and more frequent than bus or coach services.

YOU MIGHT SAY...

Is there a bus to...?
Geht ein Bus nach...?

When is the next bus to...?
Wann geht der nächste Bus nach...?

Which bus goes to the city centre?
Welcher Bus fährt ins Stadtzentrum?

Where is the bus stop?
Wo ist die Bushaltestelle?

Which stand does the coach leave from?
Von welchem Steig fährt der Reisebus?

Where can I buy tickets?
Wo kann ich Fahrscheine kaufen?

How much is it to go to...?
Wie viel kostet die Fahrt nach...?

A full/half fare, please.
Einen Fahrschein zum vollen / halben Preis, bitte.

A single/return ticket, please.
Eine Einzelfahrkarte / Rückfahrkarte, bitte.

Could you tell me when to get off?
Können Sie mir bitte sagen, wann ich aussteigen soll?

How many stops is it?
Wie viele Haltestellen sind das?

YOU MIGHT HEAR...

The number 17 goes to...
Die Linie 17 fährt nach...

The bus stop is down the road.
Die Bushaltestelle ist weiter unten an der Straße.

It leaves from stand 21.
Er fährt von Steig Nummer 21.

There's a bus every 10 minutes.
Der Bus fährt alle 10 Minuten.

You buy tickets at the machine/office.
Sie können Fahrscheine am Automaten / bei der Verkaufsstelle kaufen.

This is your stop.
Hier ist Ihre Haltestelle.

bus route **die Buslinie**	half fare **der halbe Fahrpreis**	school bus **der Schulbus**
bus lane **die Busspur**	concession **die Ermäßigung**	airport bus **der Flughafenbus**
bus station **der Busbahnhof**	wheelchair access **der Rollstuhlzugang**	tour bus **der Reisebus**
fare **der Fahrpreis**	night bus **der Nachtbus**	to catch the bus **den Bus nehmen**
full fare **der volle Fahrpreis**	shuttle bus **der Shuttlebus**	

YOU SHOULD KNOW...

You may be required to validate ("entwerten") your ticket before or as you board your bus or trolleybus.

bus
der Bus

bus shelter
das Wartehäuschen

bus stop
die Bushaltestelle

coach
der Reisebus

minibus
der Kleinbus

trolley bus
der Trolleybus

Cycling is hugely popular in Germany; there are many short-distance and long-distance routes. In city centres, signposts showing both a bicycle and a pedestrian mean that you must ride at walking speed.

YOU MIGHT SAY...

Where can I hire a bicycle?
Wo kann ich ein Fahrrad mieten?

How much is it to hire?
Wie viel kostet der Verleih?

My bike has a puncture.
Ich habe eine Reifenpanne.

Is there a cycle path nearby?
Gibt es hier in der Nähe einen Radweg?

YOU MIGHT HEAR...

Bike hire is ... per day/week.
Der Verleih ist ... pro Tag / Woche.

You must wear a helmet.
Sie müssen einen Helm tragen.

There's a cycle path from ... to...
Ein Radweg geht von ... bis...

VOCABULARY

cyclist
der Radfahrer / die Radfahrerin

mountain bike
das Mountainbike

road bike
das Rennrad

hybrid bike
das Hybridrad

bike stand
der Fahrradständer

bike rack
der Fahrradträger

child seat
der Kindersitz

cycle lane
der Fahrradweg

cycle path
der Radweg

puncture repair kit
das Reparaturkästchen

reflective vest
die Warnweste

cycling shorts
die Radlerhose

to cycle
radfahren

to go for a bike ride
eine Fahrradfahrt machen

bell
die Klingel

bike lock
das Fahrradschloss

front light
der Frontscheinwerfer

helmet
der Helm

pump
die Fahrradpumpe

reflector
der Reflektor

BICYCLE

handlebars
die Lenkstange

gears
die Gänge *mpl*

crossbar
die Querstange

saddle
der Sattel

frame
der Rahmen

brake
die Bremse

wheel
das Rad

tyre
der Radreifen

pedal
das Pedal

chain
die Kette

VOCABULARY

motorcyclist
**der Motorradfahrer /
die Motorradfahrerin**

moped
das Moped

scooter
der Roller

fuel tank
der Benzintank

handlebars
die Lenkstange

headlight
der Scheinwerfer

mudguard
der Kotflügel

kickstand
der Seitenständer

leathers
die Lederbekleidung

YOU SHOULD KNOW...

Motorcyclists must wear helmets and drive with their lights on.

boots
die Stiefel *mpl*

crash helmet
der Sturzhelm

helmet cam
die Helmkamera

leather gloves
die Lederhandschuhe
mpl

leather jacket
die Lederjacke

motorbike
das Motorrad

Germany has a well-developed, well-organized national railway system. Before boarding a local train, it's important to validate ("entwerten") your ticket: failure to do so can result in a fine. However, you don't need to validate your inter-city train ticket or your self-printed e-tickets.

YOU MIGHT SAY...

Is there a train to...?
Geht ein Zug nach...?

When is the next train to...?
Wann geht der nächste Zug nach...?

Where is the nearest metro station?
Wo ist die nächste U-Bahnstation?

Which platform does it leave from?
Von welchem Bahnsteig fährt er ab?

Which line do I take for...?
Mit welcher Linie fahre ich nach...?

A ticket to ..., please.
Eine Fahrkarte nach ..., bitte.

A return ticket to ..., please.
Eine Rückfahrkarte nach ..., bitte.

I'd like to reserve a seat please.
Ich würde gerne einen Sitzplatz buchen.

Do I have to change?
Muss ich umsteigen?

Where do I change for...?
Wo steige ich nach ... um?

Where is platform 4?
Wo ist Bahnsteig Nummer 4?

Is this the right platform for...?
Ist dies der richtige Bahnsteig für den Zug nach...?

Is this the train for...?
Ist das der Zug nach...?

Is this seat free?
Ist dieser Sitz frei?

I've missed my train!
Ich habe meinen Zug verpasst!

YOU SHOULD KNOW...

The Berlin underground (U-Bahn) system is among the most modern in Europe, and there are numerous other ways to get around the city. You can buy your tickets at home via the website or mobile app.

The next train leaves at...
Der nächste Zug fährt um ... ab.

This is the right train/platform.
Das ist der richtige Zug / Bahnsteig.

Would you like a single or return ticket?
Möchten Sie eine einfache Fahrkarte oder eine Rückfahrkarte?

You have to go to platform 2.
Sie müssen zum Bahnsteig Nummer 2 gehen.

I'm sorry, this journey is fully booked.
Es tut mir leid, der Zug ist ausgebucht.

This seat is free/taken.
Dieser Sitz ist frei / besetzt.

The restaurant car is in coach D.
Das Bordrestaurant ist in Wagen D.

You must change at...
Sie müssen in ... umsteigen.

The next stop is...
Die nächste Haltestelle ist...

Platform 4 is down there.
Bahnsteig Nummer 4 ist dort.

Change here for...
Steigen Sie hier nach ... um.

VOCABULARY

rail network
das Eisenbahnnetz

line
die Linie

e-ticket
das Online-Ticket

high-speed train
der Hochgeschwindigkeitszug

metro station
die U-Bahnstation

first-class
erste Klasse

passenger train
der Personenzug

left luggage
die Gepäckaufbewahrung

quiet coach
der Ruhebereich

freight train
der Güterzug

railcard
die Bahnkarte

seat reservation
die Sitzplatzreservierung

sleeper
der Nachtzug

single ticket
die einfache Fahrkarte

to change trains
umsteigen

coach
der Wagen

return ticket
die Rückfahrkarte

to validate a ticket
eine Fahrkarte entwerten

carriage
der Wagen

couchette
der Liegeplatz

departure board
der Anzeigetafel

guard
**der Bahnbeamte /
die Bahnbeamtin**

light railway
die S-Bahn

locomotive
die Lokomotive

luggage rack
die Gepäckablage

metro
die U-Bahn

platform
der Bahnsteig

porter
**der Gepäckträger /
die Gepäckträgerin**

restaurant car
das Bordrestaurant

signal box
das Stellwerk

sliding doors
die Schiebetüren *fpl*

ticket barrier
die Fahrkartensperre

ticket machine
der Fahrscheinautomat

ticket office
der Fahrkartenschalter

track
die Schienen *fpl*

train
der Zug

tram
die Straßenbahn

train station
der Bahnhof

validation machine
der Entwerter

I'm looking for check-in/my gate.
Ich suche meinen Check-in-Schalter / mein Gate.

I'm checking in one case.
Ich checke einen Koffer ein.

Which gate does the plane leave from?
Von welchem Gate geht mein Flug?

When does the gate open/close?
Wann beginnt / endet das Boarding?

Is the flight on time?
Ist der Flug pünktlich?

I would like a window/aisle seat, please.
Ich hätte gerne einen Sitz am Fenster / Gang.

I've lost my luggage.
Mein Gepäck ist verloren gegangen.

My flight has been delayed.
Mein Flug hat Verspätung.

I've missed my connecting flight.
Ich habe meinen Anschlussflug verpasst.

Is there a shuttle bus service?
Gibt es einen Shuttle-Service?

Check-in has opened for flight...
Der Check-in-Schalter für Flug Nummer ... ist geöffnet.

May I see your ticket/passport, please?
Kann ich bitte Ihr Ticket / Ihren Pass sehen?

How many bags are you checking in?
Wie viel Gepäck checken Sie ein?

Your luggage exceeds the maximum weight.
Sie sind über der Freigepäckmenge.

Please go to gate number...
Bitte begeben Sie sich zu Gate Nummer...

Your flight is delayed/cancelled.
Ihr Flug hat Verspätung / wurde annulliert.

Is this your bag?
Ist das Ihre Tasche?

Flight ... is now ready for boarding.
Der Flug ... ist bereit zum Einsteigen.

Last call for passenger...
Letzter Aufruf für Passagier...

airline
die Fluglinie

terminal
der Terminal

Arrivals/Departures
Ankünfte / Abflüge

security
der Sicherheitsdienst

passport control
die Passkontrolle

customs
die Zollabfertigung

cabin crew
das Flugbegleitpersonal

business class
die Business Class

economy class
die Touristenklasse

aisle
der Gang

tray table
der Klapptisch

overhead locker
das Gepäckfach

seatbelt
der Sicherheitsgurt

wing
die Tragfläche

engine
die Maschine

fuselage
der Rumpf

hold
der Frachtraum

hold luggage
das aufgegebene Gepäck

excess baggage
das Übergepäck

hand/cabin baggage
das Handgepäck

connecting flight
der Anschlussflug

jetlag
der Jetlag

to check in (online)
(Online) einchecken

YOU SHOULD KNOW...

Germany has a lot of airports, but many airlines only operate routes from the UK to major cities in Germany, so it is best to check well in advance when flights to less central destinations are available.

aeroplane
das Flugzeug

airport
der Flughafen

baggage reclaim
die Gepäckausgabe

boarding card
die Bordkarte

cabin
die Kabine

check-in desk
der Check-in-Schalter

cockpit
das Cockpit

departure board
die Anzeigetafel

duty-free shop
der Duty-free-Shop

holdall
die Reisetasche

luggage trolley
der Kofferkuli

passport
der Reisepass

pilot
der Pilot / die Pilotin

runway
die Landebahn

suitcase
der Koffer

From the northern ports of Germany, you can take ferries to Denmark, Sweden, Norway, Latvia, and Lithuania.

YOU MIGHT SAY...

When is the next boat to...?
Wann geht das nächste Boot nach...?

Where does the boat leave from?
Von wo legt das Boot ab?

What time is the last boat to...?
Wann geht das letzte Boot nach...?

How long is the trip/crossing?
Wie lange dauert die Reise / die Überfahrt?

How many crossings a day are there?
Wie viele Überfahrten gibt es am Tag?

How much for ... passengers?
Wie viel ist es für ... Passagiere?

How much does it cost for a vehicle?
Wie viel ist es für ein Auto?

I feel seasick.
Ich bin seekrank.

YOU MIGHT HEAR...

The boat leaves from...
Das Boot legt von ... ab.

The trip/crossing lasts...
Die Reise / die Überfahrt dauert...

There are ... crossings a day.
Pro Tag gibt es ... Überfahrten.

The ferry is delayed/cancelled.
Die Fähre hat Verspätung / ist annulliert.

Sea conditions are good/bad.
Die Seebedingungen sind gut / schlecht.

VOCABULARY

ferry crossing
die Überfahrt

ferry terminal
der Fährhafen

car deck
das Autodeck

deck
das Deck

port
der Hafen

crew
die Besatzung

funnel
der Schornstein

marina
der Jachthafen

foot passenger
der Fußpassagier /
die Fußpassagierin

porthole
das Bullauge

canal
der Kanal

to board
an Bord gehen

lifeboat
das Rettungsboot

coastguard
die Küstenwache

to sail
auslaufen

bow
der Bug

captain
der Kapitän /
die Kapitänin

to dock
anlegen

stern
das Heck

GENERAL

anchor
der Anker

buoy
die Boje

gangway
die Gangway

harbour
der Hafen

jetty
der Hafendamm

lifebuoy
der Rettungsring

lifejacket
die Schwimmweste

lock
die Schleuse

mooring
der Anlegeplatz

BOATS

canal boat
das Kanalboot

canoe
das Kanu

ferry
die Fähre

inflatable dinghy
das Schlauchboot

kayak
das Kajak

liner
das Passagierschiff

rowing boat
das Ruderboot

sailing boat
das Segelboot

yacht
die Jacht

IN THE HOME | IM HAUS

Germany is attracting more and more tourists and expats looking for a place to call "Zuhause" for a time, whether it's for a holiday or a longer-term stay. This could be a city-centre apartment, a cosy cottage in a rural spot, or an expansive and luxurious castle.

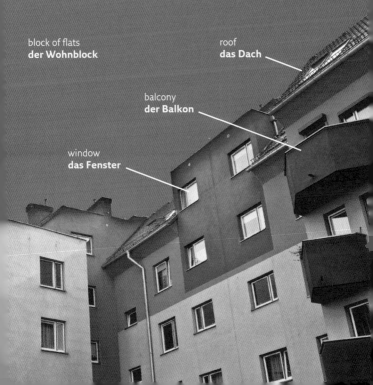

block of flats
der Wohnblock

roof
das Dach

balcony
der Balkon

window
das Fenster

Most of Germany's population lives in urban areas, although it's quite common for people to head out of the city at the weekend, perhaps to see family or explore the countryside.

YOU MIGHT SAY...

I live in...
Ich wohne in...

I've recently moved.
Ich bin vor kurzem eingezogen.

I'm staying at...
Ich wohne bei...

I'm moving to...
Ich ziehe nach...

My address is...
Meine Adresse ist...

I don't like this area.
Ich mag die Gegend nicht.

I have a flat/house.
Ich habe eine Wohnung / ein Haus.

I'd like to buy/rent a property here.
Ich würde hier gerne etwas kaufen / mieten.

I'm the homeowner/tenant.
Ich bin der Eigentümer / der Mieter.

YOU MIGHT HEAR...

Where do you live?
Wo wohnen Sie?

What's your address, please?
Wie lautet Ihre Adresse?

Where are you staying?
Bei wem wohnen Sie?

Are you the owner/tenant?
Sind Sie Eigentümer / Mieter?

How long have you lived here?
Seit wann wohnen Sie hier?

Do you like this area?
Mögen Sie diese Gegend?

YOU SHOULD KNOW...

Rental agreements and the protection available for tenants can vary according to whether the property is furnished or unfurnished; make sure you understand what your rights are if you intend to rent long term in Germany.

VOCABULARY

terraced house
das Reihenhaus

townhouse
das Stadthaus

villa
die Villa

building
das Gebäude

address
die Adresse

suburb
der Vorort

district
der Bezirk

letting agent
**der Makler /
die Maklerin**

estate agent
**der Immobilien-
händler / die
Immobilienhändlerin**

landlord
der Vermieter

landlady
die Vermieterin

tenant
**der Mieter /
die Mieterin**

neighbour
**der Nachbar /
die Nachbarin**

mortgage
die Hypothek

rent
die Miete

rental agreement
der Mietvertrag

holiday let
**die
Urlaubsvermietung**

to rent
mieten

to own
besitzen

to live
wohnen

to move house
umziehen

to build a house
ein Haus bauen

TYPES OF BUILDING

apartment block
der Wohnblock

bungalow
der Bungalow

detached house
das Einzelhaus

farmhouse
der Bauernhof

semi-detached house
das Doppelhaus

studio flat
**die
Einzimmerwohnung**

47

YOU MIGHT SAY...

We are renovating our home.
Wir renovieren unser Haus.

We are redecorating the lounge.
Wir machen das Wohnzimmer neu.

There's a problem with...
Wir haben ein Problem mit...

It's not working.
Es funktioniert nicht.

The drains are blocked.
Die Rohre sind verstopft.

The boiler has broken.
Der Boiler ist kaputt.

There's no hot water.
Wir haben kein warmes Wasser.

We have a power cut.
Der Strom ist ausgefallen.

I need a plumber/an electrician.
Ich brauche einen Klempner / einen Elektriker.

Can you recommend anyone?
Können Sie mir jemanden empfehlen?

Can it be repaired?
Ist es reparierbar?

I can smell gas/smoke.
Es riecht nach Gas / Rauch.

YOU MIGHT HEAR...

What seems to be the problem?
Was ist das Problem?

How long has it been broken/leaking?
Seit wann ist es kaputt / undicht?

Where is the meter/fuse box?
Wo ist der Stromzähler / der Sicherungskasten?

Here's a number for a plumber/an electrician.
Hier ist die Nummer für einen Klempner / einen Elektriker.

VOCABULARY

room **das Zimmer**	attic **der Dachboden**	wall **die Wand**
cellar **der Keller**	ceiling **die Decke**	floor **der Boden**

porch	plug	satellite dish
die Veranda	**der Stecker**	**die Parabolantenne**
back door	adaptor	power cut
die Hintertür	**der Adapter**	**der Stromausfall**
French windows	socket	window cleaner
die Fenstertür	**die Steckdose**	**der Fensterputzer /**
		die Fensterputzerin
balcony	electricity	
der Balkon	**die Elektrizität**	to fix
		reparieren
skylight	air conditioning	
das Oberlicht	**die Klimaanlage**	to decorate
		dekorieren
battery	central heating	
die Batterie	**die Zentralheizung**	to renovate
		renovieren

YOU SHOULD KNOW...

Tradespeople in Germany must be insured and registered, and it is the householder's responsibility to ensure that any work carried out on their property is done by a qualified supplier.

INSIDE

boiler
der Boiler

ceiling fan
der Deckenventilator

extension cable
das Verlängerungskabel

fuse box
der Sicherungskasten

heater
der Heizkörper

light bulb
die Glühbirne

meter
der Stromzähler

radiator
der Heizkörper

security alarm
der Sicherheitsalarm

smoke alarm
der Rauchmelder

thermostat
das Thermostat

wood-burning stove
der Holzofen

OUTSIDE

chimney
der Schornstein

aerial
die Antenne

gutter
die Regenrinne

drainpipe
das Abflussrohr

roof
das Dach

gable
der Giebel

garage
die Garage

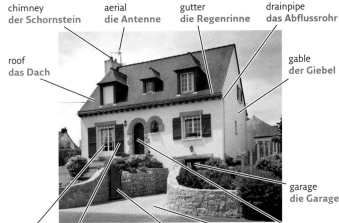

window
das Fenster

shutter
der Fensterladen

gate
das Tor

driveway
die Auffahrt

front door
die Haustür

50

YOU MIGHT SAY/HEAR...

Would you like to come round?
Wollen Sie vorbeikommen?

Hi! Come in.
Hallo! Kommen Sie rein.

Make yourself at home.
Fühlen Sie sich wie zu Hause.

Shall I take my shoes off?
Soll ich meine Schuhe ausziehen?

Can I use your bathroom?
Wo ist die Toilette?

Thanks for inviting me over.
Danke für die Einladung.

VOCABULARY

front door
die Haustür

doorway
der Eingang

hallway/corridor
der Flur

landing
der Treppenabsatz

stairwell
das Treppenhaus

staircase
die Treppe

lift
der Aufzug

doormat
die Fußmatte

key
der Schlüssel

to buzz somebody in
jemanden mit dem Summer hereinlassen

to wipe one's feet
sich die Füße abtreten

to hang one's jacket up
die Jacke aufhängen

doorbell
die Türklingel

intercom
die Sprechanlage

letterbox
der Briefkasten

VOCABULARY

carpet
der Teppich

floorboards
die Dielen *fpl*

suite
die Garnitur

sofa bed
das Schlafsofa

table lamp
die Tischlampe

home entertainment system
das Home-Entertainment-System

cable TV
das Kabelfernsehen

satellite TV
das Satellitenfernsehen

TV on demand
das Fernsehen auf Abruf

to relax
sich entspannen

to sit down
sich setzen

to watch TV
fernsehen

GENERAL

bookcase
das Bücherregal

curtains
die Vorhänge *mpl*

display cabinet
die Vitrine

DVD/Blu-ray® player
der DVD-Player / Blu-ray-Player®

radio
das Radio

remote control
die Fernbedienung

sideboard
die Anrichte

TV stand
der Fernsehschrank

Venetian blind
die Jalousie

LOUNGE

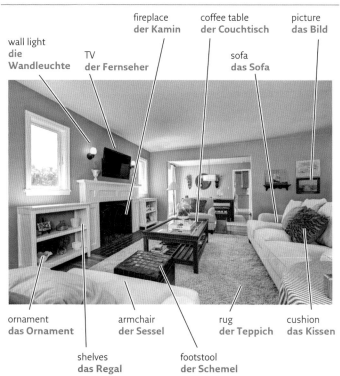

wall light
die Wandleuchte

TV
der Fernseher

fireplace
der Kamin

coffee table
der Couchtisch

picture
das Bild

sofa
das Sofa

ornament
das Ornament

armchair
der Sessel

rug
der Teppich

cushion
das Kissen

shelves
das Regal

footstool
der Schemel

Although people tend to eat in the dining room if they have one, or at a table in the lounge, many people also eat in the kitchen where there is often a corner bench.

VOCABULARY

kettle **der Kessel**	to cook **kochen**	to bake **backen**
toaster **der Toaster**	to fry **braten**	to wash up **das Geschirr spülen**
electric cooker **der Elektroherd**	to stir-fry **(unter Rühren) kurz anbraten**	to clean the worktops **die Arbeitsfläche saubermachen**
gas cooker **der Gasherd**	to boil **kochen**	to put away the groceries **die Einkäufe einräumen**
cooker hood **die Abzugshaube**	to roast **braten**	

YOU SHOULD KNOW...

In most German homes you will find appliances for cooking roasts and fish, a pressure cooker, and a large variety of baking utensils.

KITCHEN UTENSILS

baking tray
das Backblech

cafetière
die Pressfilterkanne

casserole dish
der Schmortopf

chopping board
das Hackbrett

colander
das Sieb

corkscrew
der Korkenzieher

food processor
die Küchenmaschine

frying pan
die Bratpfanne

grater
die Reibe

hand mixer
der Handmixer

kitchen knife
das Küchenmesser

ladle
der Schöpflöffel

masher
der Kartoffelstampfer

measuring jug
der Messbecher

mixing bowl
die Rührschüssel

peeler
der Schäler

rolling pin
das Nudelholz

saucepan
der Kochtopf

sieve
das Sieb

spatula
der Spachtel

tin opener
der Dosenöffner

whisk
der Schneebesen

wok
der Wok

wooden spoon
der Holzlöffel

MISCELLANEOUS ITEMS

aluminium foil
die Alufolie

bin bag
die Mülltüte

bread bin
der Brotkasten

clingfilm
die Frischhaltefolie

kitchen roll
das Küchenpapier

pedal bin
der Treteimer

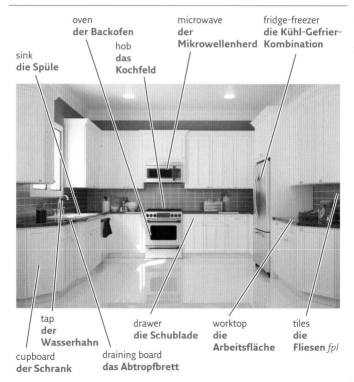

oven
der Backofen

microwave
der Mikrowellenherd

fridge-freezer
die Kühl-Gefrier-Kombination

hob
das Kochfeld

sink
die Spüle

tap
der Wasserhahn

cupboard
der Schrank

draining board
das Abtropfbrett

drawer
die Schublade

worktop
die Arbeitsfläche

tiles
die Fliesen *fpl*

VOCABULARY

dining table **der Esstisch**	crockery **das Geschirr**	to set the table **den Tisch decken**
place mat **das Set**	cutlery **das Besteck**	to dine **zu Abend essen**
coaster **der Untersetzer**	glassware **das Glasgeschirr**	to clear the table **den Tisch abräumen**

YOU SHOULD KNOW...

When dining in a German home, it is good manners always to keep your hands on the table, and to not begin eating until the host is seated and has wished you "Guten Appetit" ("enjoy your meal").

GENERAL

gravy boat
die Sauciere

napkin
die Serviette

pepper mill
die Pfeffermühle

salad bowl
die Salatschüssel

salt cellar
der Salzstreuer

serving dish
der Servierteller

bowl
die Schüssel

champagne flute
die Sektflöte

cup and saucer
die Tasse und die Untertasse

plate
der Teller

knife and fork
das Messer und die Gabel

spoon
der Löffel

teaspoon
der Teelöffel

tumbler
das Trinkglas

wine glass
das Weinglas

VOCABULARY

single bed **das Einzelbett**	en-suite bathroom **das eigene Bad**	to sleep **schlafen**
double bed **das Doppelbett**	nursery **das Kinderzimmer**	to wake up **aufwachen**
master bedroom **das Hauptschlafzimmer**	bedding **die Bettwäsche**	to make the bed **das Bett machen**
	to go to bed **ins Bett gehen**	to change the sheets **die Laken wechseln**
spare room **das Gästezimmer**		

GENERAL

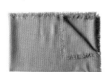

blanket
die Decke

bunk beds
das Etagenbett

clock radio
der Radiowecker

coat hanger
der Kleiderbügel

dressing table
die Frisierkommode

hairdryer
der Föhn

laundry basket
der Wäschekorb

quilt
die Bettdecke

sheets
die Laken *ntpl*

BEDROOM

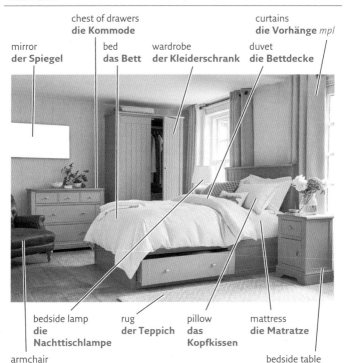

chest of drawers
die Kommode

curtains
die Vorhänge *mpl*

mirror
der Spiegel

bed
das Bett

wardrobe
der Kleiderschrank

duvet
die Bettdecke

bedside lamp
die Nachttischlampe

rug
der Teppich

pillow
das Kopfkissen

mattress
die Matratze

armchair
der Sessel

bedside table
der Nachttisch

In most German homes, toilets are situated away from the main bathroom. It is also quite common to see washing machines installed in the bathroom, rather than in the kitchen or utility room.

VOCABULARY

shower curtain
der Duschvorhang

toiletries
die Toilettenartikel
mpl

drain
der Abfluss

to shower
duschen

to have a bath
baden

to wash one's hands
sich die Hände waschen

to brush one's teeth
sich die Zähne putzen

to go to the toilet
auf die Toilette gehen

GENERAL

bath mat
die Badematte

bath towel
das Badetuch

face cloth
der Waschlappen

hand towel
das Handtuch

shower puff
der Duschpuschel

soap
die Seife

sponge
der Schwamm

toilet brush
die Klobürste

toilet roll
**die Rolle
Toilettenpapier**

BATHROOM

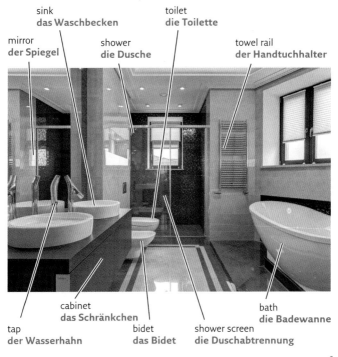

sink
das Waschbecken

toilet
die Toilette

mirror
der Spiegel

shower
die Dusche

towel rail
der Handtuchhalter

tap
der Wasserhahn

cabinet
das Schränkchen

bidet
das Bidet

shower screen
die Duschabtrennung

bath
die Badewanne

VOCABULARY

tree **der Baum**	flowerbed **das Blumenbeet**	to weed **jäten**
soil **die Erde**	compost **der Kompost**	to water **gießen**
grass **das Gras**	allotment **der Kleingarten**	to grow **anpflanzen**
plant **die Pflanze**	gardener **der Gärtner / die Gärtnerin**	to plant **pflanzen**
weed **das Unkraut**		

GENERAL

decking
die Terrasse

garden fork
die Forke

garden hose
der Gartenschlauch

gardening gloves
die Gartenhandschuhe
mpl

garden shed
das Gartenhaus

greenhouse
das Gewächshaus

hoe
die Hacke

lawnmower
der Rasenmäher

parasol
der Sonnenschirm

plant pot
der Blumentopf

pruners
die Gartenschere

spade
der Spaten

trowel
die Kelle

watering can
die Gießkanne

weedkiller
**der
Unkrautvernichter**

Wellington boots
die Gummistiefel *mpl*

wheelbarrow
der Schubkarren

window box
der Blumenkasten

lawn
der Rasen

shrub
der Strauch

gate
das Tor

fence
der Zaun

trellis
das Spalier

bird box
das Vogelhäuschen

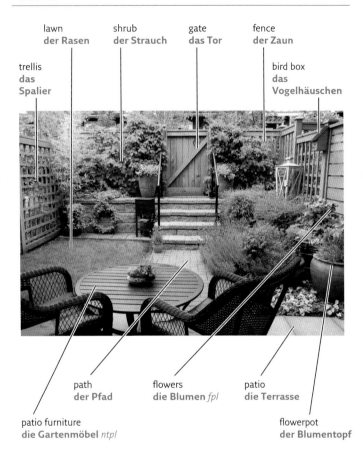

path
der Pfad

flowers
die Blumen *fpl*

patio
die Terrasse

patio furniture
die Gartenmöbel *ntpl*

flowerpot
der Blumentopf

VOCABULARY

utility room
**der Hauswirt-
schaftsraum**

household appliances
die Haushaltsgeräte
ntpl

chores
die Hausarbeit

basin
das Becken

recycling bin
der Recyclingbehälter

wastepaper basket
der Papierkorb

bleach
die Bleiche

disinfectant
**das
Desinfektionsmittel**

dishwasher tablet
**das
Spülmaschinentab**

laundry detergent
das Waschmittel

washing-up liquid
das Spülmittel

to sweep the floor
kehren

to do the laundry
die Wäsche waschen

to hoover
staubsaugen

to tidy up
aufräumen

to clean
reinigen

brush
der Besen

bucket
der Eimer

cloth
der Lappen

clothes horse
der Wäscheständer

clothes pegs
die Wäscheklammern
fpl

dishwasher
**die Geschirr-
spülmaschine**

dustbin
der Mülleimer

dustpan
die Kehrschaufel

iron
das Bügeleisen

ironing board
das Bügelbrett

mop
der Mop

rubber gloves
die Gummihandschuhe
mpl

scourer
der Topfreiniger

tea towel
das Geschirrtuch

tumble drier
der Wäschetrockner

vacuum cleaner
der Staubsauger

washing line
die Wäscheleine

washing machine
die Waschmaschine

AT THE SHOPS | IM LADEN

Markets full of lush produce and local specialities, the aroma of freshly baked bread from the Bäckerei, and the smell of roast sausage coming from a food stall – just some of the things that might spring to mind when it comes to shopping in Germany. That's not to say that you won't find plenty of large supermarkets, busy shopping centres, and many familiar international chains in urban areas too.

basket
der Korb

banana
die Banane

bread
das Brot

vegetable oil
das Pflanzenöl

Shops in Germany are open from Monday to Saturday and are closed on Sundays and on bank holidays. Opening times are regulated by each "Land" (region) – some of them allow late opening hours, while others don't. Be aware that a lot of shops close at 7 p.m. A few times a year there is "verkaufsoffener Sonntag" – Sunday opening.

YOU MIGHT SAY...

Where is the...?
Wo ist der / die / das...?

Where is the nearest...?
Wo ist der / die / das nächste...?

Where can I buy...?
Wo kann ich ... kaufen?

What time do you open/close?
Um wieviel Uhr öffnen /
schließen Sie?

I'm just looking, thanks.
Danke, ich schaue mich nur um.

Do you sell...?
Haben Sie...?

May I have...?
Kann ich bitte ... haben?

Can I pay by cash/card?
Kann ich bar / mit Karte zahlen?

Can I pay with my mobile app?
Kann ich über meine App zahlen?

How much does this cost?
Wie viel kostet das?

How much is delivery?
Wie viel kostet die Lieferung?

I need...
Ich brauche...

I would like...
Ich hätte gerne...

Can I exchange this?
Kann ich das umtauschen?

Can I get a refund?
Können Sie mir das Geld
zurückerstatten?

That's all, thank you.
Das wäre alles, danke.

YOU SHOULD KNOW...

Distribution of single-use plastic bags is banned in German shops – many stores have introduced reusable bags that can be purchased.

Can I help you?
Kann ich Ihnen helfen?

How would you like to pay?
Wie möchten Sie bezahlen?

Are you being served?
Werden Sie schon bedient?

Can you enter your PIN?
Bitte geben Sie ihre PIN ein.

Would you like anything else?
Möchten Sie sonst noch etwas?

Would you like a receipt?
Möchten Sie eine Quittung?

It costs...
Es kostet...

We don't offer refunds/exchanges.
Wir erstatten kein Geld zurück / wir tauschen nicht um.

I'm sorry, we don't have...
Es tut mir leid, wir haben kein / keine...

Have you got a receipt?
Haben Sie eine Quittung?

I can order that for you.
Ich kann es für Sie bestellen.

Have a good day!
Schönen Tag!

VOCABULARY

shop
der Laden

change
das Wechselgeld

voucher
der Gutschein

supermarket
der Supermarkt

contactless
kontaktlos

groceries
die Lebensmittel *ntpl*

shopping centre
das Einkaufszentrum

gift voucher
der Geschenkgutschein

to browse
sich umsehen

shop assistant
der Verkäufer / die Verkäuferin

loyalty card
die Paybackkarte

to buy
kaufen

customer
der Kunde / die Kundin

PIN
die PIN

to pay
zahlen

market
der Markt

exchange
der Umtausch

to shop (online)
(Online) einkaufen

cash
das Bargeld

refund
die Rückerstattung

to go shopping
einkaufen gehen

banknotes
die Banknoten *fpl*

card reader
der Kartenleser

coins
die Münzen *fpl*

debit/credit card
**die Bankkarte /
Kreditkarte**

paper bag
die Papiertüte

plastic bag
die Plastiktüte

reusable shopping bag
**die
wiederverwendbare
Einkaufstasche**

receipt
die Quittung

till point
die Kasse

Shopping for groceries over the internet is less prevalent in Germany than in the UK, but it is a growing trend. Online shopping and delivery services are offered by most German supermarkets, but availability will vary from region to region. Bear in mind that it is rare to find 24-hour shops and supermarkets, even in the biggest cities in Germany.

YOU MIGHT SAY...

Where can I find...?
Wo kann ich ... finden?

I'm looking for...
Ich suche...

Do you have...?
Haben Sie...?

YOU MIGHT HEAR...

We have/don't have...
Wir haben / haben kein / keine...

It's in aisle 1/2/3.
Es ist im Gang Nummer 1 / 2 / 3.

There is a charge for a carrier bag.
Tüten kosten extra.

VOCABULARY

aisle **der Gang**	jar **das Einmachglas**	frozen **tiefgefroren**
delicatessen **das Feinkostgeschäft**	multipack **der Multipack**	dairy **Milch-**
ready meal **das Fertiggericht**	packet **das Päckchen**	low-fat **fettarm**
bottle **die Flasche**	tin **die Dose**	low-calorie **kalorienarm**
box **die Schachtel**	tinned **konserviert**	gluten-free **glutenfrei**
carton **der Pappkarton**	fresh **frisch**	

YOU SHOULD KNOW...

At some German supermarkets, you might find an adjacent "Getränkemarkt" which sells all types of soft and alcoholic beverages.

basket
der Korb

scales
die Waage

trolley
der Einkaufswagen

GROCERIES

biscuits
die Kekse *mpl*

couscous
der Couscous

herbs
die Kräuter *ntpl*

honey
der Honig

icing sugar
der Puderzucker

instant coffee
der lösliche Kaffee

jam
die Marmelade

ketchup
das Ketchup

marmalade
**die
Orangenmarmelade**

mayonnaise
die Mayonnaise

mustard
der Senf

noodles
die Nudeln *fpl*

olive oil
das Olivenöl

pasta
die Nudeln *fpl*

pepper
der Pfeffer

rice
der Reis

salt
das Salz

sugar
der Zucker

teabags
die Teebeutel *mpl*

vegetable oil
das Pflanzenöl

vinegar
der Essig

SNACKS

chocolate
die Schokolade

crisps
die Kartoffelchips
mpl

nuts
die Nüsse *fpl*

olives
die Oliven *fpl*

popcorn
das Popcorn

sweets
die Süßigkeiten *fpl*

DRINKS

beer
das Bier

fizzy drink
die Limo

fruit juice
der Fruchtsaft

mineral water
das Mineralwasser

spirits
die Spirituosen *pl*

wine
der Wein

Most markets will be set up early in the morning and will wind down around 2 p.m., although some bigger markets can stay open all day. There you will find a wealth of fresh produce, regional specialities, and organic foods.

YOU MIGHT SAY...

Where is the market?
Wo ist der Markt?

When is market day?
Wann ist Markttag?

Two/Three ..., please.
Zwei / Drei ..., bitte.

What do I owe you?
Wie viel macht das?

YOU MIGHT HEAR...

The market is in the square.
Der Markt ist auf dem Platz.

The market is on a Tuesday.
Der Markt ist dienstags.

Here you go. Anything else?
Bitteschön. Sonst noch etwas?

Here's your change.
Hier ist Ihr Wechselgeld.

VOCABULARY

marketplace **der Marktplatz**	stall **der Stand**	local **örtlich**
flea market **der Flohmarkt**	trader **der Händler / die Händlerin**	organic **bio**
indoor market **die Markthalle**	produce **die Produkte** ntpl	seasonal **saisonbedingt**
farmer's market **der Bauernmarkt**		home-made **selbstgemacht**

YOU SHOULD KNOW...

Haggling would be considered bad form at the stalls of a fruit and vegetable market; it's a different story at the flea market!

YOU MIGHT SAY...

Where can I buy...?
Wo kann ich ... kaufen?

Do you have...?
Haben Sie...?

A kilo/100 grams of...
Ein Kilo / 100 Gramm...

YOU MIGHT HEAR...

What would you like?
Was darf es sein?

Here you go. Anything else?
Bitteschön. Sonst noch etwas?

VOCABULARY

greengrocer's der Gemüseladen	segment der Schnitz	unripe unreif
juice der Saft	skin die Schale	seedless kernlos
leaf das Blatt	stone der Kern	to chop hacken
peel die Schale	raw roh	to dice würfeln
pip der Obstkern	fresh frisch	to grate raspeln
rind die Schale	rotten verfault	to juice entsaften
seed der Kern	ripe reif	to peel schälen

YOU SHOULD KNOW...

Remember that when buying fruit or vegetables from the supermarket, customers are usually required to weigh and sticker their purchases before going to the checkouts.

apple
der Apfel

apricot
die Aprikose

banana
die Banane

blackberry
die Brombeere

blackcurrant
**die schwarze
Johannisbeere**

blueberry
die Blaubeere

cherry
die Kirsche

gooseberry
die Stachelbeere

grape
die Weintraube

grapefruit
die Grapefruit

kiwi fruit
die Kiwi

lemon
die Zitrone

mango
die Mango

melon
die Melone

orange
die Orange

passion fruit
die Passionsfrucht

peach
der Pfirsich

pear
die Birne

pineapple
die Ananas

plum
die Pflaume

raspberry
die Himbeere

redcurrant
**die rote
Johannisbeere**

strawberry
die Erdbeere

watermelon
die Wassermelone

artichoke
die Artischocke

asparagus
der Spargel

aubergine
die Aubergine

beetroot
die Rote Beete

broccoli
der Brokkoli

Brussels sprout
der Rosenkohl

cabbage
der Kohl

carrot
die Karotte

cauliflower
der Blumenkohl

celery
der Sellerie

chilli
der Chili

courgette
die Zucchini

cucumber
die Gurke

garlic
der Knoblauch

green beans
die grünen Bohnen *fpl*

leek
der Lauch

lettuce
der Blattsalat

mushroom
der Pilz

onion
die Zwiebel

peas
die Erbsen

potato
die Kartoffel

red pepper
der rote Paprika

spinach
der Spinat

tomato
die Tomate

YOU MIGHT SAY...

How fresh is this fish?
Wie frisch ist dieser Fisch?

I'd like this filleted, please.
Ich hat ihn gerne filetiert.

YOU MIGHT HEAR...

Would you like this filleted?
Hätten Sie ihn gerne filetiert?

Shall I remove the bones?
Soll ich entgräten?

VOCABULARY

fishmonger
**der Fischhändler /
die Fischhändlerin**

(fish)bone
die Gräte

fillet
das Filet

roe
der Rogen

scales
die Schuppen *fpl*

shellfish
das Schalentier

shell
die Schale

freshwater
Süßwasser-

saltwater
Meereswasser-

farmed
gezüchtet

wild
wild

salted
gesalzen

smoked
geräuchert

deboned
entgrätet

filleted
filetiert

YOU SHOULD KNOW...

Fishmongers often serve bread rolls with fish fillings, for a quick bite to eat.

FISH

anchovy
die Sardelle

cod
der Kabeljau

eel
der Aal

haddock
der Schellfisch

herring
der Hering

lemon sole
die Seezunge

mackerel
die Makrele

monkfish
der Seeteufel

salmon
der Lachs

sardine
die Sardine

sea bream
die Brasse

skate
der Rochen

trout
die Forelle

tuna
der Thunfisch

zander
der Zander

clam
die Venusmuschel

crab
die Krabbe

crayfish
die Languste

lobster
der Hummer

mussel
die Miesmuschel

octopus
der Kraken

oyster
die Auster

prawn
die Garnele

scallop
die Jakobsmuschel

sea urchin
der Seeigel

shrimp
die Garnele

squid
der Tintenfisch

Butchers in Germany are often able to recommend what kind of cuts to buy for the recipes you'd like to try, as well as local specialities they may sell.

YOU MIGHT SAY...

A slice of ..., please.
Eine Scheibe ..., bitte.

Can you slice this for me, please?
Könnten Sie es bitte in Scheiben schneiden?

YOU MIGHT HEAR...

How much would you like?
Wie viel möchten Sie?

How many would you like?
Wie viele möchten Sie?

VOCABULARY

butcher
der Metzger /
die Metzgerin

meat
das Fleisch

red/white meat
das rote /
weiße Fleisch

cold meats
der Aufschnitt

veal
das Kalbfleisch

beef
das Rindfleisch

venison
das Rehfleisch

game
das Wild

duck
die Ente

goose
die Gans

lamb
das Lammfleisch

turkey
das Putenfleisch

pork
das Schweinefleisch

offal
die Innereien

joint
das Bratenstück

frankfurter
das Würstchen

pâté
die Pastete

organic
bio

raw
roh

cooked
gebraten

YOU SHOULD KNOW...

Germany is well known for its Wurst – sausages – and its Aufschnitt – cold meats. They can be made from all kinds of meat and can be cured, boiled, or smoked. Leberwurst, Blutwurst, Landjäger, Teewurst... as long as you aren't vegetarian, there's one for every taste.

bacon
der Speck

beefburger
der Hamburger

bratwurst
die Bratwurst

chicken
das Hähnchen

chop
das Kotelett

ham
der Schinken

meatloaf
der Leberkäse

mince
das Hackfleisch

ribs
die Rippchen *ntpl*

sausage
die Wurst

schnitzel
das Schnitzel

steak
das Steak

Bread and bread rolls are a German speciality. Bakeries offer up to a dozen different kinds of bread rolls and a whole range of breads, from dark wholemeal to French baguette. A "Bäckerei" sells bread and a "Konditorei" sells cakes and pastries. Often, however, both are combined in the same shop.

YOU MIGHT SAY...

What time do you open/close?
Um wieviel Uhr öffnen / schließen Sie?

Do you sell...?
Haben Sie...?

Could I have...?
Kann ich bitte ... haben?

How much are...?
Was kosten...?

YOU MIGHT HEAR...

Are you being served?
Werden Sie schon bedient?

Would you like anything else?
Möchten Sie sonst noch etwas?

It costs...
Es kostet...

I'm sorry, we don't have...
Es tut mir leid, wir haben kein / keine...

VOCABULARY

baker
der Bäcker / die Bäckerin

bread
das Brot

wholemeal bread
das Vollkornbrot

loaf
der Brotlaib

baguette
das Baguette

croissant
das Croissant

slice
das Stück

crust
die Kruste

dough
der Teig

flour
das Mehl

gluten-free
glutenfrei

to bake
backen

YOU SHOULD KNOW...

You can also find bakery products in some service stations and train stations.

apple strudel
der Apfelstrudel

black forest gateau
**die Schwarzwälder
Kirschtorte**

bread rolls
die Brötchen *ntpl*

cheesecake
der Käsekuchen

Danish pastry
das Plundergebäck

doughnut
der Berliner

fruit tart
die Obsttorte

lebkuchen
der Lebkuchen

marzipan
das Marzipan

pancakes
die Pfannkuchen
mpl

pretzel
die Brezel

stollen
der Stollen

VOCABULARY

egg white
das Eiweiß

egg yolk
das Eigelb

double cream
der Doppelrahm

sour cream
die saure Sahne

margarine
die Margarine

UHT milk
die H-Milch

pasteurized milk
die pasteurisierte Milch

unpasteurized milk
die Rohmilch

whole milk
die Vollmilch

skimmed milk
die Magermilch

semi-skimmed milk
die Halbfettmilch

caged
aus Käfighaltung

free-range
aus Freilandhaltung

dairy-free
milchfrei

butter
die Butter

cream
die Sahne

egg
das Ei

milk
die Milch

soymilk
die Sojamilch

yoghurt
der Joghurt

Germans are no strangers to the pleasure of eating a good cheese board. Specialist cheesemongers carry a wide variety of international cheeses, while there is always a good choice at the supermarket cheese counter.

VOCABULARY

blue cheese	cream cheese	curd cheese
der Blauschimmelkäse	**der Frischkäse**	**der Quark**

Appenzeller
der Appenzeller

Camembert
der Camembert

Emmenthal
der Emmental

goat's cheese
der Ziegenkäse

mozzarella
der Mozzarella

parmesan
der Parmesan

Roquefort
der Roquefort

smoked cheese
der Räucherkäse

Tilsit cheese
der Tilsiter

In Germany, pharmacies are owned and run by individual pharmacists, which means that you don't see pharmacy chains in German towns and villages. There are also several chains of "Drogeriemarkt" (drugstores) that sell non-pharmaceuticals, cosmetics and hygiene products, organic foodstuffs, and sometimes wine.

YOU MIGHT SAY...

I need something for...
Ich brauche etwas für...

I'm allergic to...
Ich bin allergisch gegen...

I'm collecting a prescription.
Ich hole ein Rezept ab.

What would you recommend?
Was empfehlen Sie mir?

Is it suitable for young children?
Ist es für Kleinkinder geeignet?

YOU MIGHT HEAR...

Do you have a prescription?
Haben Sie ein Rezept?

Do you have any allergies?
Leiden Sie an Allergien?

Take two tablets every day.
Nehmen Sie zwei Tabletten täglich.

You should see a doctor.
Sie sollten zum Arzt gehen.

I'd recommend...
Ich empfehle Ihnen...

VOCABULARY

pharmacist
**der Apotheker /
die Apothekerin**

prescription
das Rezept

cold
die Erkältung

diarrhoea
der Durchfall

hay fever
der Heuschnupfen

headache
die Kopfschmerzen
mpl

sore throat
die Halsschmerzen
mpl

stomachache
die Magenschmerzen
mpl

antihistamine
**das
Antihistaminikum**

antiseptic
das Antiseptikum

decongestant
**das abschwellende
Mittel**

painkiller
das Schmerzmittel

handwash
**die
Hand-Waschlotion**

antiseptic cream
die antiseptische Salbe

bandage
der Verband

capsule
die Kapsel

condom
das Kondom

cough mixture
der Hustensaft

drops
die Tropfen *mpl*

insect repellent
das Insekten-schutzmittel

lozenge
die Pastille

medicine
die Medizin

plaster
das Pflaster

suntan lotion
die Sonnencreme

tablet/pill
die Tablette

conditioner
die Pflegespülung

dental floss
die Zahnseide

mouthwash
das Mundwasser

razor
der Rasierer

sanitary towel
die Damenbinde

shampoo
das Shampoo

shaving foam
der Rasierschaum

shower gel
das Duschgel

soap
die Seife

tampon
der Tampon

toothbrush
die Zahnbürste

toothpaste
die Zahnpasta

blusher
das Rouge

comb
der Kamm

eyeliner
der Eyeliner

eyeshadow
der Lidschatten

foundation
die Grundlage

hairbrush
die Haarbürste

hairspray
das Haarspray

lip balm
der Lippenbalsam

lipstick
der Lippenstift

mascara
die Mascara

nail varnish
der Nagellack

powder
der Puder

If you intend to travel to Germany with your baby, it may be possible to hire the equipment you require from specialist companies.

VOCABULARY

colic	bubble bath	to be teething
die Kolik	**das Schaumbad**	**zahnen**
disposable nappy	nappy rash	to breast-feed
die Wegwerfwindel	**die Windeldermatitis**	**stillen**

CLOTHING

Babygro®/sleepsuit	bib	bootees
der Babyschlafanzug	**das Lätzchen**	**die Babyschühchen**
		ntpl

mittens	snowsuit	vest
die Fausthandschuhe	**der Schneeanzug**	**der Body**
mpl		

baby food
die Babynahrung

baby lotion
die Babylotion

baby's bottle
die Babyflasche

changing bag
die Wickeltasche

cotton bud
das Wattestäbchen

cotton wool
die Watte

formula milk
die Formel

nappy
die Windel

nappy cream
die Windelcreme

rusk
der Zwieback

talcum powder
der Körperpuder

wet wipes
die Feuchttücher
ntpl

baby bath
die Babywanne

baby seat
die Babyschale

baby walker
das Lauflerngerät

cot
das Kinderbett

dummy
der Schnuller

highchair
der Hochstuhl

mobile
das Mobile

Moses basket
der Moseskorb

pram
der Kinderwagen

pushchair
der Sportwagen

teething ring
der Beißring

travel cot
das Reisebett

As well as newspapers and magazines, German newsagents may also sell tobacco, stamps, and tickets for local public transport.

VOCABULARY

broadsheet **die großformatige Zeitung**	tabloid **die Boulevardzeitung**	vendor **der Verkäufer / die Verkäuferin**
kiosk **der Kiosk**	tobacconist **der Tabakwarenladen**	daily **täglich**
stationery **die Schreibwaren** *fpl*		weekly **wöchentlich**

GENERAL

book
das Buch

cigar
die Zigarre

cigarette
die Zigarette

comic book
das Comicheft

confectionery
die Süßigkeiten *fpl*

envelope
der Briefumschlag

greetings card
die Grußkarte

magazine
die Zeitschrift

map
die Landkarte

newspaper
die Zeitung

notebook
das Notizbuch

pen
der Kugelschreiber

pencil
der Bleistift

postcard
die Postkarte

puzzle book
das Rätselbuch

scratch card
das Rubbellos

stamp
die Briefmarke

tobacco
der Tabak

If you fancy a shopping spree in Berlin, the city has the biggest department store in mainland Europe – only Harrods is bigger! There are, of course, many other, smaller department stores and shopping malls that offer all the international brands as well as German fashion designers.

YOU MIGHT SAY...

Where is the menswear department?
Wo ist die Herrenabteilung?

Which floor is this?
In welchem Stockwerk sind wir?

Can you gift-wrap this, please?
Können Sie das bitte als Geschenk verpacken?

What a bargain!
Das ist aber günstig!

YOU MIGHT HEAR...

Menswear is on the second floor.
Die Herrenabteilung ist im zweiten Stock.

This is the first floor.
Hier ist der erste Stock.

Would you like this gift-wrapped?
Möchten Sie eine Geschenkverpackung?

VOCABULARY

brand
die Marke

counter
die Theke

escalator
die Rolltreppe

lift
der Fahrstuhl

toilets
die Toilette

floor
die Etage

department
die Abteilung

menswear
die Herrenbekleidung

womenswear
die Damenbekleidung

sportswear
die Sportkleidung

swimwear
die Badebekleidung

sale
der Ausverkauf

to be on sale
verkauft werden

to be in the sale
im (Sonder)angebot sein

accessories
die Modeaccessoires
ntpl

cosmetics
die Kosmetika

fashion
die Mode

food and drink
die Lebensmittel *ntpl*

footwear
die Schuhe *mpl*

furniture
die Möbel *ntpl*

kitchenware
die Küchengeräte
ntpl

leather goods
die Lederwaren *fpl*

lighting
die Beleuchtung

lingerie
die Damenwäsche

soft furnishings
die Wohntextilien *fpl*

toys
das Spielzeug

The Kurfürstendamm, known as Ku'damm by the locals, is Berlin's favourite shopping street, with famous designer boutiques and great cafés. Bikini Berlin is Germany's first "concept mall" where you can find all sorts of interesting boutiques, restaurants, and pop-ups.

YOU MIGHT SAY...

I'm just looking, thanks.
Danke, ich schaue mich nur um.

I'd like to try this on, please.
Ich würde das gerne anprobieren.

Where are the fitting rooms?
Wo sind die Umkleidekabinen?

I'm a size...
Ich habe Größe...

Have you got a bigger/smaller size?
Haben Sie es größer / kleiner?

This is too small/big.
Das ist zu klein / groß.

This is torn.
Das ist zerrissen.

It's not my style.
Es ist nicht mein Stil.

YOU MIGHT HEAR...

Can I help you?
Kann ich Ihnen helfen?

Let me know if I can help.
Sagen Sie mir Bescheid, falls Sie Hilfe brauchen.

The fitting rooms are over there.
Die Umkleidekabinen sind dort drüben.

What size are you?
Welche Größe haben Sie?

I'm sorry, it's out of stock.
Es tut mir leid, es ist ausverkauft.

I'm sorry, we don't have that size/colour.
Es tut mir leid, wir haben diese Größe / Farbe nicht mehr.

That suits you.
Das steht Ihnen gut.

VOCABULARY

fitting room **die Umkleidekabine**	shoes/footwear **die Schuhe** *mpl*	umbrella **der (Regen)schirm**
clothes/clothing **die Kleidung**	underwear **die Unterwäsche**	jewellery **der Schmuck**

scent	cotton	petite
das Parfüm	**die Baumwolle**	**kleine Größe**
casual	leather	plus-size
lässig	**das Leder**	**Übergrößen-**
smart	silk	to try on
schick	**die Seide**	**anprobieren**
wool	size	to fit
die Wolle	**die Größe**	**passen**

CLOTHING

bikini
der Bikini

blouse
die Bluse

boxer shorts
die Boxershorts *pl*

bra
der Büstenhalter

cardigan
die Strickjacke

coat
der Mantel

dress
das Kleid

dressing gown
der Bademantel

dungarees
die Latzhose

jacket
die Jacke

jeans
die Jeans *pl*

jogging bottoms
die Jogginghose

jumper
der Pullover

leggings
die Leggings *pl*

pants
die Unterhose

pyjamas
der Schlafanzug

shirt
das Hemd

shorts
die Shorts *pl*

skirt
der Rock

socks
die Socken *fpl*

suit
das Kostüm

sweatshirt
das Sweatshirt

swimsuit
der Badeanzug

three-piece suit
der Dreiteiler

tie
die Krawatte

tights
die Strumpfhose

trousers
die Hose

T-shirt
das T-Shirt

waistcoat
die Weste

waterproof jacket
die Regenjacke

baseball cap
die Baseballmütze

belt
der Gürtel

bracelet
das Armband

braces
die Hosenträger *mpl*

earrings
die Ohrringe *mpl*

gloves
die Handschuhe *mpl*

handbag
die Handtasche

necklace
die Halskette

purse
der Geldbeutel

scarf
der Schal

wallet
die Brieftasche

woolly hat
die Wollmütze

boots
die Stiefel *mpl*

court shoes
die Pumps *mpl*

high heels
die Stöckelschuhe
mpl

lace-up shoes
die Schnürschuhe *mpl*

plimsolls
die Strandschuhe *mpl*

sandals
die Sandalen *fpl*

slippers
die Pantoffeln *fpl*

trainers
die Sportschuhe *mpl*

Wellington boots
die Gummistiefel *mpl*

DIY is popular in Germany. From local retail and trade merchants to numerous larger chain stores, there are many options available for those who are looking for some DIY essentials.

VOCABULARY

electricity **die Elektrizität**	decorating **das Tapezieren**	power tool **das Elektrowerkzeug**
joinery **die Tischlerei**	plumbing **die Klempnerarbeiten** *fpl*	toolbox **der Werkzeugkasten**
home improvements **das Heimwerken, das DIY**	tool **das Werkzeug**	to do DIY **heimwerken**
painting **das Streichen**		

chisel
der Meißel

electric drill
die Bohrmaschine

hammer
der Hammer

nails
die Nägel *mpl*

nuts and bolts
die Muttern und Bolzen *pl*

paint
die Farbe

paintbrush
der Pinsel

paint roller
der Farbroller

pliers
die Zange

saw
die Säge

screwdriver
der Schraubenzieher

screws
die Schrauben *fpl*

spanner
der Schraubenschlüssel

spirit level
die Wasserwaage

stepladder
die Trittleiter

tiles
die Fliesen *fpl*

wallpaper
die Tapete

wrench
der Schraubenschlüssel

antique shop
**die Antiquitäten-
handlung**

barber's
der Herrenfriseur

beauty salon
der Kosmetiksalon

bookmaker's
der Buchmacher

bookshop
der Buchladen

boutique
die Boutique

car showroom
das Autohaus

electrical retailer
**der
Elektrofachmarkt**

estate agency
das Immobilienbüro

florist's
der Blumenladen

furniture store
der Möbelmarkt

garden centre
das Gartencenter

hairdresser's
der Frisör

health food shop
das Reformhaus

jeweller's
das Juweliergeschäft

music shop
der Musikladen

off-licence
die Wein- und Spirituosenhandlung

optician's
der Optiker

pet shop
die Tierhandlung

phone shop
der Handy-Shop

shoe shop
das Schuhgeschäft

shopping mall
das Shoppingcenter

toyshop
das Spielwarengeschäft

travel agency
das Reisebüro

DAY-TO-DAY | DER ALLTAG

Business meetings, meals with friends, or courses of study... whatever your day-to-day schedule looks like during your time in Germany, you will require some basic vocabulary when going on errands, planning outings, and going about your everyday business.

coffee with milk
der Milchkaffee

handle
der Henkel

cup
die Tasse

saucer
die Untertasse

Here are a few basic words and phrases for describing your day-to-day routine ("der Alltag"), and making plans with others.

YOU MIGHT SAY...

Where are you going?
Wo gehen Sie hin?

What time do you finish?
Wann hören Sie auf?

What are you doing today/tonight?
Was machen Sie heute / heute Abend?

Are you free on Friday?
Sind Sie am Freitag frei?

Would you like to meet up?
Sollen wir uns treffen?

Where/When would you like to meet?
Wo / Um wie viel Uhr sollen wir uns treffen?

I can't meet up then, sorry.
Es tut mir leid, ich kann in dem Moment nicht.

YOU MIGHT HEAR...

I'm at work/uni.
Ich bin bei der Arbeit / auf der Uni.

I have a day off.
Ich habe frei.

I've got an appointment.
Ich bin verabredet.

I'm going to...
Ich gehe nach / zu...

I'll be back by...
Ich komme gegen ... Uhr zurück.

I'll meet you at 6 p.m.
Ich komme um 18 Uhr nach.

I'll meet you at the restaurant.
Ich treffe Sie im Restaurant.

VOCABULARY

to wake up **aufwachen**	to leave **weggehen**	to meet friends **sich mit Freunden treffen**
to get dressed **sich anziehen**	to study **studieren**	to go home **nach Hause gehen**
to arrive **ankommen**	to work **arbeiten**	to go to bed **ins Bett gehen**

In Germany, breakfast is an important meal. It often includes a choice of cold meats, cheese, and eggs, as well as quark (a type of cottage cheese), jam, and honey.

VOCABULARY

breakfast bar **die Frühstückstheke**	quark **der Quark**	to spread **aufstreichen**
bread and butter **das Butterbrot**	fried eggs **die Spiegeleier** *ntpl*	to have breakfast **frühstücken**
bread and jam **das Marmeladenbrot**	poached eggs **die verlorene Eier** *ntpl*	to skip breakfast **das Frühstück überspringen**

boiled eggs
die gekochten Eier *ntpl*

bread rolls
die Brötchen *ntpl*

cereal
die Frühstückscerealien *pl*

coffee
der Kaffee

coffee with milk
der Milchkaffee

cold meats and cheese
der Aufschnitt und der Käse

croissant
das Croissant

honey
der Honig

hot chocolate
der Kakao

jam
die Marmelade

orange juice
der Orangensaft

rye bread
das Roggenbrot

muesli
das Müsli

scrambled eggs
die Rühreier *ntpl*

tea
der Tee

Traditionally, lunch was the main meal of the day in Germany. These days some people still have a big lunch during their lunch break and a lighter meal in the evenings, while others prefer to have their main meal later on in the day.

YOU MIGHT SAY...

What's for dinner?
Was gibt es zum Abendessen?

What time is lunch?
Wann essen wir zu Mittag?

Can I try it?
Darf ich probieren?

YOU MIGHT HEAR...

Lunch is at midday.
Das Mittagessen ist um zwölf.

Dinner's ready!
Zu Tisch!

Would you like...?
Möchten Sie...?

VOCABULARY

food **das Essen**	courses **die Gänge** *mpl*	to eat/drink **essen / trinken**
drink **das Getränk**	recipe **das Rezept**	to have lunch **zu Mittag essen**
lunch **das Mittagessen**	aperitif **der Aperitif**	to have dinner **speisen**
dinner **das Abendessen**	after-dinner drink **der Digestif**	to eat out **zum Essen ausgehen**

STARTERS

asparagus wrapped in ham
der Spargel mit Schinken

cold meats
der Aufschnitt

green salad
der grüne Salat

mixed salad
der gemischte Salat

omelette
das Omelett

onion tart
der Zwiebelkuchen

pâté
die Pastete

smoked salmon
der Räucherlachs

soup
die Suppe

SIDES

chips
die Pommes *ntpl*

cucumber salad
der Gurkensalat

fried potatoes
die Bratkartoffeln
ntpl

German dumplings
die Klöße *mpl*

gratin
der Auflauf

mash
der Kartoffelbrei

noodles
die Nudeln *fpl*

pasta
die Nudeln *fpl*

potatoes
die Kartoffeln *fpl*

potato fritters
die Kartoffelpuffer *mpl*

rice
der Reis

vegetables
das Gemüse

CLASSIC GERMAN DISHES

beef olives
die Rinderrouladen
fpl

chicken fricassee
das Hühnerfrikassee

fried and marinated
herring
der Brathering

gammon with
sauerkraut
**das Kassler mit
Sauerkraut**

goulash soup
die Gulaschsuppe

meatballs
die Frikadellen *fpl*

pancake soup
die Fritattensuppe

pea soup
die Erbsensuppe

pork knuckle with sauerkraut
das Eisbein auf Sauerkraut

pot roast
der Sauerbraten

ravioli
die Maultaschen *fpl*

stuffed cabbage leaves
die Kohlrouladen *fpl*

schnitzel
das Schnitzel

apple strudel
der Apfelstrudel

apple tart
der Apfelkuchen

blancmange
der Pudding

chocolate cake
der Schokoladenkuchen

fruit tart
die Obsttorte

ice cream
das Eis

red fruit compote
die rote Grütze

shredded pancake
der Kaiserschmarrn

syllabub
die Weinschaumcreme

YOU MIGHT SAY...

I'd like to make a reservation.
Ich würde gerne reservieren.

A table for four, please.
Einen Tisch für vier Personen, bitte.

What would you recommend?
Was empfehlen Sie mir?

What are the specials today?
Was ist das Tagesgericht?

May I have ..., please?
Kann ich bitte ... haben?

Are there vegetarian/vegan options?
Haben Sie ein Menü für Vegetarier / Veganer?

I'm allergic to...
Ich bin allergisch gegen...

Excuse me, this is cold.
Entschuldigen Sie, das ist kalt.

This is not what I ordered.
Das habe ich nicht bestellt.

May we have the bill, please?
Die Rechnung, bitte.

YOU MIGHT HEAR...

At what time?
Um wie viel Uhr?

How many people?
Für wie viele Personen?

Sorry, we're fully booked.
Es tut mir leid, wir sind voll.

Would you like anything to drink?
Möchten Sie etwas zu trinken?

Are you ready to order?
Möchten Sie bestellen?

I'd recommend...
Ich empfehle Ihnen...

The specials today are...
Wir haben heute folgende Tagesgerichte...

I will let the chef know.
Ich gebe es an den Koch weiter.

Enjoy your meal!
Guten Appetit!

VOCABULARY

set menu	daily specials	service charge
das Tagesmenü	**die Tagesgerichte** *ntpl*	**die Bedienung**

tip
das Trinkgeld

wine waiter
**der Weinkellner /
die Weinkellnerin**

barman/barmaid
**der Barkeeper / die
Bardame**

vegetarian
vegetarisch

vegan
veganisch

gluten-free
glutenfrei

dairy-free
milchfrei

to reserve a table
**einen Tisch
reservieren**

to order
bestellen

to ask for the bill
**die Rechnung
verlangen**

to be served
bedient werden

YOU SHOULD KNOW...

Some restaurants put free bread on the table, sometimes with butter.
But beware if the waiter asks you if you want bread – you might find it on
the bill later!

bar
die Bar

bill
die Rechnung

bread basket
der Brotkorb

chair
der Stuhl

champagne flute
das Sektglas

cheese knife
das Käsemesser

fish knife
das Fischmesser

jug of water
der Krug Wasser

menu
die Speisekarte

napkin
die Serviette

salt and pepper
das Salz und der Pfeffer

steak knife
das Steakmesser

table
der Tisch

tablecloth
die Tischdecke

toothpicks
die Zahnstocher *mpl*

vinegar and oil
der Essig und das Öl

waiter/waitress
der Kellner / die Kellnerin

wine glass
das Weinglas

Fast food may not be the first thing you think of when it comes to German dining, but there are plenty of options for eating on the go.

YOU MIGHT SAY...

I'd like to order, please.
Ich würde gerne bestellen.

Do you deliver?
Liefern Sie?

I'm sitting in/taking away.
**Zum hier Essen /
Zum Mitnehmen.**

That's everything, thanks.
Danke, das wäre alles.

YOU MIGHT HEAR...

Can I help you?
Kann ich Ihnen helfen?

Sit-in or takeaway?
**Zum hier Essen oder zum
Mitnehmen?**

We do/don't do delivery.
Wir liefern / Wir liefern nicht.

Would you like anything else?
Möchten Sie sonst noch etwas?

VOCABULARY

fast-food chain
die Fastfood-Kette

food stall
der Schnellimbiss

street food
das Streetfood

vendor
**der Verkäufer /
die Verkäuferin**

drive-thru
das Drive-In

an order to go/
a takeaway
zum Mitnehmen

delivery charge
die Lieferkosten pl

delivery man/woman
**der Lieferant /
die Lieferantin**

to phone in an order
**eine Bestellung
telefonisch
aufgeben**

to place an order
bestellen

to collect an order
**die Bestellung
abholen**

YOU SHOULD KNOW...

There are many food stalls to choose from if you fancy a quick bite to eat: Brezel, Bratwurst, or Currywurst stalls are common features on German street corners.

baked potato
die gefüllte Kartoffel

bratwurst
die Bratwurst

burger
der Hamburger

fries
die Pommes frites
ntpl

kebab
der Kebab

omelette
das Omelett

pizza
die Pizza

pretzel
die Brezel

sandwich
das Sandwich

sausage with curry
sauce
die Currywurst

sushi
die Sushis *ntpl*

wrap
der Wrap

Technology plays a huge role in people's everyday lives. A mere click, tap, or swipe helps us to stay in touch with friends and family, keep up to date with what's going on, and find the information we need.

YOU MIGHT SAY/HEAR...

I'll give you a call later.
Ich rufe Sie später an.

I'll text/email you.
Ich schicke Ihnen eine E-Mail / eine SMS.

This is a bad line.
Der Empfang ist sehr schlecht.

I don't have any signal.
Ich habe keinen Empfang.

What's your number/email address?
Was ist ihre Telefonnummer / E-Mail-Adresse?

The website address is...
Die Webadresse ist...

What's the WiFi password?
Was ist das WLAN-Passwort?

It's all one word.
Das wird zusammengeschrieben.

It's upper/lower case.
Das ist großgeschrieben / kleingeschrieben.

VOCABULARY

post	link	icon
der Beitrag	**der Link**	**das Icon**
social media	internet	mouse
die sozialen Netzwerke *ntpl*	**das Internet**	**die Maus**
	WiFi	mouse mat
email	**das WLAN**	**das Mauspad**
die E-Mail		
	website	keyboard
email address	**die Website**	**die Tastatur**
die E-Mail-Adresse		

app
die App

voice mail
die Voicemail

to send a text/an email
eine SMS / E-Mail schicken

data
die Daten *ntpl*

touchscreen
der Touchscreen

to post (online)
posten

mobile phone
das Handy

monitor
der Bildschirm

to download/upload
herunterladen / hochladen

landline
das Festnetz

button
die Taste

to click on
anklicken

phone call
der Anruf

battery
der Akku

to charge your phone
das Handy aufladen

text message
die SMS

cable
das Kabel

phone signal
das Handy-Signal

to make a phone call
anrufen

to switch on/off
einschalten / ausschalten

charger
das Ladegerät

computer
der Computer

SIM card
die SIM-Karte

smartphone
das Smartphone

tablet
das Tablet

wireless router
der WLAN-Router

Compulsory education in Germany begins at the age of six or seven. The minimum school-leaving age is determined by each "Land".

YOU MIGHT SAY...

What are you studying?
Was studierst du?

What year are you in?
In welchem Jahr bist du?

What's your favourite subject?
Was ist dein Lieblingsfach?

Do you have any homework?
Hast du Hausaufgaben?

YOU MIGHT HEAR...

I'm studying...
Ich studiere...

I'm in Year 6/my final year.
Ich bin im sechsten / letzten Jahr.

I enjoy...
Ich mag...

I have an assignment.
Ich muss eine Arbeit schreiben.

VOCABULARY

nursery school
der Kindergarten

primary school
die Grundschule

secondary school
die weiterführende Schule

college
die Hochschule

university
die Universität

headteacher
der Schulleiter / die Schulleiterin

teacher
der Lehrer / die Lehrerin

pupil
der Schüler / die Schülerin

janitor
der Hausmeister / die Hausmeisterin

classroom
das Klassenzimmer

timetable
der Stundenplan

lesson
die Unterrichtsstunde

lecture
der Vortrag

tutorial
das Tutorial

homework
die Hausaufgaben *fpl*

assignment
die Aufgabe

exam
die Prüfung

degree
der Hochschul- / Studienabschluss

undergraduate
der Student / die Studentin

postgraduate
der Graduierte / die Graduierte

canteen
die Kantine

assembly hall
die Aula

playing field
das Spielfeld

playground
der Schulhof

halls of residence
die Studenten-wohnheime *ntpl*

student union
das Studentenwerk

student card
der Studentenausweis

to learn
lernen

to read
lesen

to write
schreiben

to teach
unterrichten

to revise
(den Stoff) wiederholen

to sit an exam
eine Prüfung ablegen

to graduate
den Abschluss machen

to study
studieren

SCHOOL

colouring pencils
die Farbstifte *mpl*

eraser
der Radierer

exercise book
das Heft

paper
das Papier

pen
der Kugelschreiber

pencil
der Bleistift

pencil case
die Federmappe

ruler
das Lineal

schoolbag
die Schultasche

sharpener
der Anspitzer

textbook
das Lehrbuch

whiteboard
die Weißwandtafel

HIGHER EDUCATION

cafeteria
die Cafeteria

campus
der Campus

lecture hall
der Hörsaal

lecturer
**der Dozent /
die Dozentin**

library
die Bibliothek

student
**der Student /
die Studentin**

Office hours tend to be from 8 a.m. to 6 p.m., with a lunch break of at least half an hour. At lunchtime, if you want to eat at your office desk rather than going out for lunch, you must get permission from your employer.

YOU MIGHT SAY/HEAR...

Can we arrange a meeting?
Können wir einen Termin ausmachen?

May I speak to...?
Könnte ich bitte mit ... sprechen?

I have a meeting with...
Ich habe einen Termin mit...

I'll email the files to you.
Ich schicke Ihnen die Dateien per E-Mail.

Mr/Ms ... is on the phone.
Herr / Frau ... ist am Telefon.

Here's my business card.
Hier ist meine Visitenkarte.

Who's calling?
Wer spricht, bitte?

Can I call you back?
Kann ich Sie zurückrufen?

VOCABULARY

manager
der Chef / die Chefin

staff
die Mitarbeiter *mpl*

client
der Kunde / die Kundin

supplier
der Lieferant / die Lieferantin

colleague
der Kollege / die Kollegin

human resources
die Personalabteilung

accounts
die Buchhaltung

figures
die Zahlen *fpl*

spreadsheet
die Tabellenkalkulation

presentation
der Vortrag

report
der Bericht

meeting
die Sitzung

conference call
das Konferenzgespräch

video conference
die Videokonferenz

ink cartridge
die Tintenpatrone

inbox
der Posteingang

file
die Datei

attachment
der Anhang

password
das Passwort

to give a presentation
einen Vortrag halten

upgrade
das Upgrade

to type
Maschine schreiben

to hold a meeting
eine Sitzung einberufen

username
der Benutzername

to log on/off
einloggen / ausloggen

calculator
der Taschenrechner

desk
der Schreibtisch

desk lamp
die Schreibtischlampe

filing cabinet
der Aktenschrank

folder
die Mappe

hole punch
der Locher

in/out tray
die Ablage für Eingänge / Ausgänge

laptop
der Laptop

notepad
der Notizblock

paper clip
die Heftklammer

photocopier
das Fotokopiergerät

printer
der Drucker

ring binder
das Ringbuch

scanner
der Scanner

scissors
die Schere

stapler
der Hefter

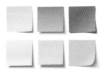

sticky notes
die Post-it-Notizen
fpl

sticky tape
das Klebeband

swivel chair
der Drehstuhl

telephone
das Telefon

USB stick
der USB-Stick

German banks have variable business hours from Monday to Friday. They are usually closed on Saturdays, and sometimes even on Friday afternoons.

YOU MIGHT SAY...

I'd like to...
Ich würde gerne...

... open an account.
... ein Konto eröffnen.

... apply for a loan/mortgage.
... ein Darlehen / einen Immobilienkredit beantragen.

... register for online banking.
... für das Online-Banking anmelden.

Is there a fee for this service?
Gibt es Gebühren?

I need to cancel my debit/credit card.
Ich muss meine Bankkarte / Kreditkarte kündigen.

YOU MIGHT HEAR...

May I see your ID, please?
Kann ich bitte Ihren Ausweis sehen?

How much would you like to withdraw/deposit?
Wie viel wollen Sie abheben / einzahlen?

Could you enter your PIN, please?
Geben Sie bitte ihre PIN ein.

You must fill out an application form.
Sie müssen ein Formular ausfüllen.

You must make an appointment.
Sie müssen einen Termin ausmachen.

There is a fee for this service.
Es gibt Gebühren.

VOCABULARY

branch
die Zweigstelle

cashier
der Kassierer / die Kassierin

online banking
das Online-Banking

bank account
das Bankkonto

current account
das Girokonto

savings account
das Sparkonto

account number
die Kontonummer

bank statement
der Kontoauszug

bank balance
der Kontostand

overdraft	loan	to repay
die Kontoüberziehung	**das Darlehen**	**zurückzahlen**
bank transfer	mortgage	to withdraw
die Überweisung	**die Hypothek**	**abheben**
chequebook	interest	to make a deposit
das Scheckheft	**die Zinsen** *pl*	**Geld einzahlen**
currency	to borrow	to change money
die Währung	**einen Kredit aufnehmen**	**Geld wechseln**

ATM
der Geldautomat

banknotes
die Banknoten *fpl*

bureau de change
die Wechselstube

debit/credit card
die Bankkarte / Kreditkarte

exchange rate
der Wechselkurs

safety deposit box
der Safe

Opening hours for post offices will vary from place to place, so check what times the local branch opens and closes. Be aware that some postboxes will have one slot for local mail and one for destinations further afield.

YOU MIGHT SAY...

I'd like to send this first-class/ by airmail.
Ich möchte das als Expressbrief / Luftpost aufgeben.

Can I get a certificate of postage, please?
Kann ich bitte einen Nachweis haben?

How long will delivery take?
Wie lange braucht die Zustellung?

I'd like a book of stamps, please.
Ein Heftchen Briefmarken, bitte.

YOU MIGHT HEAR...

Place it on the scales, please.
Legen Sie es bitte auf die Waage.

What are the contents?
Was enthält es?

What is the value of this parcel?
Wie viel ist es wert?

That comes to ..., please.
Das macht ..., bitte.

Would you like a certificate of postage?
Wollen sie einen Nachweis?

How many stamps do you require?
Wie viele Briefmarken wollen Sie?

VOCABULARY

address **die Adresse**	airmail **die Luftpost**	to send **schicken**
postal van **das Postfahrzeug**	first-class **prioritär**	to receive mail **Post bekommen**
courier **der Kurier**	second-class **Standard**	to return a package **ein Paket zurückschicken**
mail **die Post**	to post **einwerfen**	

box
die Schachtel

envelope
der Briefumschlag

letter
der Brief

package
das Paket

padded envelope
die Luftpolstertasche

postal worker
**der Postangestellte /
die Postangestellte**

postbox
der Briefkasten

postcard
die Postkarte

stamp
die Briefmarke

YOU MIGHT SAY...

How do I get to the city centre?
Wie komme ich ins Stadtzentrum?

I'd like to visit...
Ich würde gerne ... besichtigen.

I need to go to...
Ich muss zu... / nach...

What are the opening hours?
Was sind die Öffnungszeiten?

YOU MIGHT HEAR...

It's open between ... and...
Es ist zwischen ... und... geöffnet.

It's closed on Mondays.
Montag ist geschlossen.

PLACES OF IMPORTANCE

café
das Café

cathedral
die Kathedrale

church
die Kirche

conference centre
das Kongresszentrum

courthouse
das Gerichtsgebäude

fire station
die Feuerwache

fountain
der Springbrunnen

hospital
das Krankenhaus

hotel
das Hotel

laundrette
der Waschsalon

library
die Bibliothek

mosque
die Moschee

office block
das Bürogebäude

park
der Park

playground
der Spielplatz

police station
die Polizeiwache

synagogue
die Synagoge

town hall
das Rathaus

A day trip, a break away, a night out, maybe even a night in – we all like to spend our free time differently. It's also a common topic of conversation with friends and colleagues; who doesn't like talking about holidays, hobbies, and how they like to hang out?

tent
das Zelt

guy rope
die Zeltleine

flysheet
das Überzelt

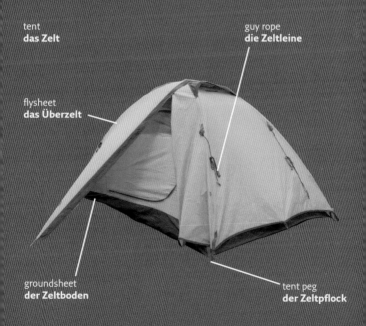

groundsheet
der Zeltboden

tent peg
der Zeltpflock

YOU MIGHT SAY...

What would you like to do?
Was möchten Sie tun?

What do you do in your spare time?
Was machen Sie in Ihrer Freizeit?

Have you got any hobbies?
Haben Sie Hobbys?

Do you enjoy...?
Mögen Sie...?

Are you sporty/creative/musical?
Sind Sie sportlich / kreativ / musikalisch?

Are you going on holiday this year?
Machen Sie dieses Jahr Urlaub?

How often do you go...?
Wie oft gehen Sie...?

YOU MIGHT HEAR...

My hobbies are...
Meine Hobbys sind...

I like going to the theatre.
Ich gehe gern ins Theater.

I really enjoy it.
Ich mag es sehr.

It's not for me.
Das ist nichts für mich.

I'm going on holiday.
Ich mache Urlaub.

I have/don't have a lot of spare time.
Ich habe / Ich habe nicht viel Freizeit.

VOCABULARY

holiday
der Urlaub

spare time
die Freizeit

activity
die Aktivität

hobby/pastime
das Hobby

to be interested in something
sich für etwas interessieren

to be keen on doing something
etwas gern tun

to pass the time
die Zeit vertreiben

to relax
sich entspannen

to enjoy
genießen

to be bored
sich langweilen

cooking
das Kochen

DIY
das Heimwerken

gaming
Videospiele spielen

gardening
die Gartenarbeit

jogging
das Jogging

listening to music
Musik hören

reading
das Lesen

shopping
das Einkaufen

sports
der Sport

travelling
das Reisen

walking
das Laufen

watching TV/films
**fernsehen /
Filme sehen**

Germany has a lot to offer as a tourist destination from the picturesque castle of Neuschwanstein to cycling trips through the Rhine valley.

YOU MIGHT SAY...

How much is it to get in?
Wie viel kostet der Eintritt?

Is there a discount for students/ seniors?
Gibt es eine Ermäßigung für Studenten / Senioren?

Where is the tourist office?
Wo ist das Fremdenverkehrsamt?

Are there sightseeing tours?
Gibt es Rundfahrten?

Are there audio guides available?
Haben Sie Audioguides?

YOU MIGHT HEAR...

Entry costs...
Der Eintritt kostet...

There is/isn't a discount available.
Es gibt / Es gibt keine Ermäßigung.

The tourist office is located...
Das Fremdenverkehrsamt ist...

You can book a guided tour.
Sie können eine Rundfahrt buchen.

Audio guides are/are not available.
Es gibt / Es gibt keine Audioguides.

VOCABULARY

tourist **der Tourist / die Touristin**	nature reserve **das Naturschutzgebiet**	audio guide **der Audioguide**
tourist attraction **die Touristenattraktion**	historic site **die historische Stätte**	to visit **besichtigen** to see **sehen**
excursion **der Ausflug**	guided tour **die Rundfahrt**	to book **buchen**

YOU SHOULD KNOW...

Some cultural and historical sites, such as museums, art galleries, and castles, are closed on certain days of the week (usually Mondays).

art gallery
die Kunstgalerie

camera
die Kamera

castle
das Schloss

cathedral
die Kathedrale

city map
der Stadtplan

gardens
der Garten

guidebook
der Reiseführer

monument
das Denkmal

museum
das Museum

sightseeing bus
der Sightseeing-Bus

tour guide
**der Reiseführer /
die Reiseführerin**

tourist office
**das Fremdenver-
kehrsbüro**

When it comes to nightlife in Germany's towns and cities, check the local tourist office for information on local events and venues. Why not get recommendations on bars and clubs from residents, too?

YOU MIGHT SAY...

What is there to do at night?
Was kann man abends machen?

What's on at the cinema/theatre?
Was gibt es im Kino / im Theater?

Where are the best bars/clubs?
Wo sind die besten Kneipen / Clubs?

Do you want to go for a drink?
Wollen Sie etwas trinken gehen?

Do you want to go and see a film/show?
Möchten Sie einen Film / ein Theaterstück sehen?

Are there tickets for...?
Gibt es Karten für...?

Two seats in the stalls/balcony, please.
Zwei Parkettplätze / zwei Rangplätze, bitte.

What time does it start?
Wann fängt es an?

I enjoyed myself.
Ich habe viel Spaß gehabt.

YOU MIGHT HEAR...

The nightlife is/isn't great around here.
Das Nachtleben ist hier / ist hier nicht besonders lebendig.

My favourite bar/club is...
Meine Lieblingsbar / Mein Lieblingsclub ist...

I'm going for a few drinks/to the theatre.
Ich gehe einen trinken / ins Theater.

There's a film/show I'd like to see.
Da gibt es einen Film, / eine Vorstellung, den / die ich gerne sehen würde.

There are tickets left.
Es gibt noch Karten.

There are no tickets left.
Es gibt keine Karten mehr.

It begins at 7 o'clock.
Es fängt um 19 Uhr an.

Please turn off your mobile phones.
Bitte schalten Sie Ihre Handys aus.

Did you have a good night?
Hatten Sie einen schönen Abend?

VOCABULARY

a drink **ein Glas**	film **der Film**	to see a show **sich eine Vorführung ansehen**
nightlife **das Nachtleben**	festival **die Festspiele**	to watch a film **sich einen Film ansehen**
party **die Party**	box office **die Kasse**	to go dancing **tanzen gehen**
show **die Vorführung**	to socialize **Kontakte knüpfen**	to enjoy oneself **sich amüsieren**
play **das (Theater)stück**	to order food/drinks **zu essen / zu trinken bestellen**	

YOU SHOULD KNOW...

Many bars and restaurants in German towns and cities have outdoor terraces ideal for people-watching; however, waiters often object to customers rearranging tables to suit their group, so let them make the arrangements for you.

ballet
das Ballett

bar
die Bar

carnival
der Karneval

casino
das Kasino

cinema
das Kino

comedy show
die Comedy-Show

concert
das Konzert

funfair
der Jahrmarkt

musical
das Musical

nightclub
der Nachtclub

opera
die Oper

restaurant
das Restaurant

theatre
das Theater

Germany welcomes an increasing flow of visitors every year, and there's a vast range of accommodation available, from high-end hotels to cosy bed and breakfasts.

YOU MIGHT SAY...

Have you got rooms available?
Haben Sie freie Zimmer?

How much is it per night?
Wie viel kostet es pro Nacht?

Is breakfast included?
Ist das Frühstück inbegriffen?

Is there a city tax?
Muss man eine Kurtaxe zahlen?

I'd like to check in, please.
Ich würde gerne einchecken.

I'd like to check out, please.
Ich möchte auschecken.

What time is breakfast served?
Um wie viel Uhr gibt es Frühstück?

I have a reservation.
Ich habe gebucht.

I'd like to book a single/double room, please.
Ich möchte ein Einzelzimmer / Doppelzimmer buchen.

What time do I have to check out?
Um wie viel Uhr muss ich das Zimmer räumen?

Could I upgrade my room?
Kann ich ein Zimmer-Upgrade haben?

I need fresh towels/more soap for my room.
Ich brauche neue Handtücher / mehr Seife in meinem Zimmer.

I've lost my key.
Ich habe den Schlüssel verloren.

I'd like to make a complaint.
Ich möchte eine Beschwerde einlegen.

YOU SHOULD KNOW...

When checking in to your hotel, you may be expected to fill out a registration form ("der Meldeschein") and provide your passport number.

We don't have any rooms available.
Wir haben keine freien Zimmer.

Our rates are...
Es kostet...

Breakfast is/is not included.
Das Frühstück ist / ist nicht inbegriffen.

Breakfast is served at...
Frühstück gibt es um ... Uhr.

May I have your room number, please?
Kann ich bitte Ihre Zimmernummer haben?

May I see your documents, please?
Ihre Papiere, bitte.

You may check in after...
Sie können ab ... Uhr ankommen.

You must check out before...
Sie müssen das Zimmer vor ... Uhr räumen.

VOCABULARY

bed and breakfast
die Frühstückspension

full board
die Vollpension

half board
die Halbpension

"vacancies"
„Zimmer frei"

room service
der Zimmerservice

wake-up call
der Weckruf

room number
die Zimmernummer

per person per night
pro Person pro Nacht

to check in
einchecken

to check out
auschecken

to order room service
Zimmerservice bestellen

corridor
der Korridor

"do not disturb" sign
das „Bitte nicht stören"-Schild

double room
das Doppelzimmer

key card
die Schlüsselkarte

minibar
die Minibar

porter
**der Gepäckträger /
die Gepäckträgerin**

reception
**der
Empfangsbereich**

receptionist
**der Empfangschef /
die Empfangschefin**

safe
der Tresor

single room
das Einzelzimmer

toiletries
die Toilettenartikel
mpl

twin room
das Zweibettzimmer

There are a vast number of campsites in Germany, offering different types of accommodation and facilities for travellers. Some "Länder" have options for wild camping ("das Wildcampen"), but you must check what the local and national restrictions are before you set off on your trip.

YOU MIGHT SAY...

Have you got spaces available?
Haben Sie freie Plätze?

I'd like to book for ... nights.
Ich möchte für ... Nächte buchen.

Can we camp here?
Dürfen wir hier ein Zelt aufschlagen?

How much is it per night?
Wie viel kostet es pro Nacht?

Where is the toilet/shower block?
Wo ist die Toilette / der Duschraum?

Is the water drinkable?
Ist das Wasser trinkbar?

YOU MIGHT HEAR...

We don't have any spaces.
Wir haben keine freien Plätze.

You can camp here.
Sie können hier Zelte aufschlagen.

It costs ... per night.
Es kostet ... pro Nacht.

The toilets/showers are located...
Die Toiletten / die Duschräume sind...

The water is/is not drinkable.
Das Wasser ist / ist nicht trinkbar.

VOCABULARY

campsite **der Campingplatz**	toilet/shower block **die Toilette / der Duschraum**	to camp **zelten**
pitch **der Platz**	camper **der Camper / die Camperin**	to pitch/take down a tent **ein Zelt aufschlagen / abbrechen**
electricity hook-up **der Stromanschluss**	"no camping" **„Zelten verboten"**	

YOU SHOULD KNOW...

All caravans and motorhomes on German motorways have to pay a toll.

air bed
die Luftmatratze

barbecue
der Grill

camping stove
der Campingkocher

caravan
der Wohnwagen

cool box
die Kühlbox

fold-up chair
der Campingstuhl

matches
die Streichhölzer
ntpl

motorhome
der Camper

picnic blanket
die Picknick-Decke

sleeping bag
der Schlafsack

tent
das Zelt

torch
die Taschenlampe

Germany has almost 1,500 miles of coastline along the North Sea and the Baltic Sea. The coast is a popular holiday destination, with long sandy beaches where kitesurfing is a favourite activity. There, you will also find the very typical "Strandkörbe", lockable beach chairs made of wicker, wood, and canvas.

YOU MIGHT SAY...

Is there a good beach nearby?
Gibt es hier in der Nähe einen schönen Strand?

Is swimming permitted here?
Darf man hier baden?

Is the water cold?
Ist das Wasser kalt?

Can we hire...?
Kann man ... mieten?

YOU MIGHT HEAR...

This is a public/private beach.
Das ist ein öffentlicher / privater Strand.

Swimming is allowed/forbidden.
Baden ist gestattet / verboten.

Swimming is/is not supervised.
Das Baden ist / ist nicht überwacht.

The water is warm/freezing!
Das Wasser ist angenehm / eisig!

VOCABULARY

"No swimming." **„Baden verboten."**	suntan **die Sonnenbräune**	to swim **schwimmen**
bathing zone **das Badegebiet**	to sunbathe **in der Sonne liegen**	

YOU SHOULD KNOW...

Public beaches are often monitored and may use a flag system to indicate bathing conditions:
Yellow-and-red – "safe for swimming"
Yellow – "no bathing for non-swimmers"
Red – "danger – no lifeguards present"
Black-and-white – "reserved for watersports".
If you see a sign saying "FKK-Strand" or "FKK-Badeort", you should expect a nudist beach. You may encounter nude sunbathers on "normal" beaches too.

THE SEASIDE

sand
der Sand

sea
das Meer

waves
die Wellen *fpl*

parasol
der Sonnenschirm

sunbed
die Sonnenliege

beach towel
das Strandtuch

GENERAL

beach ball
der Wasserball

beach hut
das Strandhäuschen

bikini
der Bikini

bucket and spade
der Eimer und die Schaufel

deckchair
der Liegestuhl

flip-flops
die Flip-Flops *mpl*

flippers
die Flossen *fpl*

promenade
die Promenade

sandcastle
die Sandburg

seashells
die Muscheln *fpl*

seaweed
der Seetang

snorkel
der Schnorchel

sunglasses
die Sonnenbrille

sunhat
der Sonnenhut

suntan lotion
die Sonnencreme

swimming trunks
die Badehose

swimsuit
der Badeanzug

windbreak
der Windschutz

YOU MIGHT SAY...

I enjoy listening to music.
Ich höre gern Musik.

I play...
Ich spiele...

I'm learning to play...
Ich lerne, ... zu spielen.

What kind of music do you like?
Welche Art Musik hören Sie gerne?

Is there a live music scene here?
Wo kann man hier Live-Musik hören?

YOU MIGHT HEAR...

I like/don't like...
Ich mag / mag nicht...

My favourite group is...
Meine Lieblingsband ist...

There's a good music scene here.
Es gibt hier eine gute LiveMusik-Szene.

YOU SHOULD KNOW...

June 21st is Fête de la Musique (Music Day), celebrated worldwide and first established in France in 1981. It has kept its French name in Germany. Munich was the first German city to organize the event, and now many free concerts and music events are held throughout the country on this date.

VOCABULARY

DJ
der DJ

CD
die CD

vinyl record
die Schallplatte

microphone
das Mikrofon

song
das Lied

album
das Album

singer-songwriter
der Singer-Songwriter / die Singer-Songwriterin

band
die Band

live music
die Livemusik

gig
der Gig

pop
der Pop

| folk music | rap | to sing |
| die Folkmusik | der Rap | singen |

| rock | classical | to listen to music |
| der Rock | klassisch | Musik hören |

| hip-hop | to play an instrument | to go to gigs |
| der Hip-Hop | ein Instrument spielen | auf Konzerte gehen |

EQUIPMENT

Bluetooth® speaker
der Bluetooth®-Lautsprecher

earphones
die Ohrhörer *mpl*

headphones
die Kopfhörer *pl*

soundbar
die Soundbar

speakers
die Lautsprecher *mpl*

turntable
der Plattenspieler

MUSICAL INSTRUMENTS

accordion
das Akkordeon

acoustic guitar
die Akustikgitarre

bass drum
die große Trommel

bass guitar
der E-Bass

cello
das Cello

clarinet
die Klarinette

cymbals
das Becken

double bass
der Kontrabass

electric guitar
die E-Gitarre

flute
die Flöte

harp
die Harfe

keyboard
das Keyboard

mouth organ
die Mundharmonika

piano
das Klavier

saxophone
das Saxophon

snare drum
die kleine Trommel

trombone
die Posaune

trumpet
die Trompete

tuba
die Tuba

violin
die Geige

xylophone
das Xylophon

GENERAL

choir
der Chor

conductor
**der Dirigent /
die Dirigentin**

musician
**der Musiker /
die Musikerin**

orchestra
das Orchester

sheet music
die Noten *fpl*

singer
**der Sänger /
die Sängerin**

YOU MIGHT SAY...

Can I take photos here?
Darf ich hier Fotos machen?

Where can I print my photos?
Wo kann ich Fotos ausdrucken lassen?

YOU MIGHT HEAR...

Photography isn't allowed.
Fotografieren ist verboten.

Say cheese!
Bitte lächeln!

VOCABULARY

photo
das Foto

photographer
**der Fotograf /
die Fotografin**

selfie
das Selfie

selfie stick
der Selfie-Stick

to take a photo/selfie
**ein Foto / Selfie
machen**

to zoom in
heranzoomen

camera lens
das Objektiv

compact camera
die Kompaktkamera

drone
die Drohne

DSLR camera
die DSLR-Kamera

SD card
**die
SD-Speicherkarte**

tripod
das Stativ

Board game cafés ("Spiel-Café") where you can get together over a drink and a favourite board game are starting to appear across Germany – they make for great opportunities to use and improve your German!

YOU MIGHT SAY...

Shall we play a game?
Sollen wir ein Spiel spielen?

What would you like to play?
Was möchtest du / möchtet ihr spielen?

What are the rules?
Was sind die Spielregeln?

YOU MIGHT HEAR...

It's your turn.
Du bist dran.

Time's up!
Die Zeit ist um.

Shall we play something else?
Können wir etwas anderes spielen?

VOCABULARY

player
**der Spieler /
die Spielerin**

hide and seek
das Versteckspiel

crossword
das Kreuzworträtsel

solitaire
die Patience

poker
das Poker

hand (in cards)
das Blatt

games console
die Spielekonsole

video game
das Videospiel

to play
spielen

to roll the dice
würfeln

to win
gewinnen

to lose
verlieren

backgammon
das Backgammon

board game
das Brettspiel

bowling
das Bowling

cards
die Karten *fpl*

chess
das Schachspiel

counters
die Spielsteine *mpl*

darts
die Darts

dice
der Würfel

dominoes
das Dominospiel

draughts
das Damespiel

jigsaw puzzle
das Puzzle

skittles
das Kegelspiel

There has been a growing interest in arts and crafts pursuits over the last number of years in Germany, with more and more craft fairs appearing across the country. Painting, sculpting, and pottery holidays are also increasingly popular.

VOCABULARY

handicrafts **das Kunsthandwerk**	amateur **der Amateur / die Amateurin**	to sketch **skizzieren**
craft fair **der Kunsthandwerksmarkt**	dressmaker **der Schneider / die Schneiderin**	to sew **nähen**
artist **der Künstler / die Künstlerin**	to paint **malen**	to knit **stricken**
		to be creative **kreativ sein**

GENERAL CRAFTS

embroidery
die Stickerei

jewellery-making
die Schmuckherstellung

model-making
der Modellbau

papercrafts
die Papierbastelei

pottery
die Töpferei

woodwork
die Holzarbeit

canvas
die Leinwand

easel
die Staffelei

ink
die Tinte

oil paint
die Ölfarbe

paintbrush
der Pinsel

palette
die Palette

paper
das Papier

pastels
die Pastellfarben *fpl*

pen
der Kugelschreiber

pencil
der Bleistift

sketchpad
der Skizzenblock

watercolours
die Wasserfarben *fpl*

ball of wool
der Knäuel

buttons
die Knöpfe *mpl*

crochet hook
die Häkelnadel

fabric
der Stoff

fabric scissors
die Stoffschere

knitting needles
die Stricknadeln *fpl*

needle and thread
die Nadel und der Faden

pins
die Stecknadeln *fpl*

safety pin
die Sicherheitsnadel

sewing basket
der Nähkorb

sewing machine
die Nähmaschine

tape measure
das Maßband

SPORT | DER SPORT

Be it football or ice hockey, cycling or skiing, Germany has a long sporting history. There are hundreds of sports and fitness clubs, plus events across the country that you can get involved with, either as a player or as a spectator. You may be looking to participate in a sport, head to the gym, or you may simply want to chat about how "die Mannschaft" is getting on.

football pitch
das Spielfeld

centre circle
der Mittelkreis

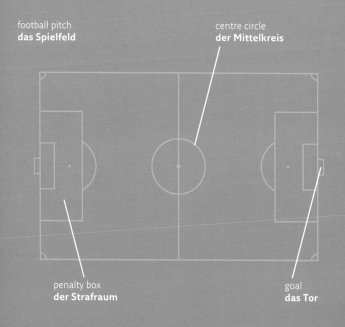

penalty box
der Strafraum

goal
das Tor

YOU MIGHT SAY...

I like keeping active.
Ich bin gerne aktiv.

Where is the nearest...?
Wo ist der / die / das nächste...?

I train ... times per week.
Ich trainiere ... Mal pro Woche.

I play football/hockey.
Ich spiele Fußball / Hockey.

I'd like to book...
Ich würde gern ... reservieren.

YOU MIGHT HEAR...

Do you do any sports?
Treiben Sie Sport?

Where/When do you train?
Wo / Wann trainieren Sie?

Do you follow any sports?
Verfolgen Sie einen bestimmten Sport?

What's your favourite team?
Welche ist Ihre Lieblingsmannschaft?

I'm a fan of...
Ich bin Fan von...

VOCABULARY

tournament
das Turnier

competition
der Wettbewerb

league
die Meisterschaft

champion
der Meister / die Meisterin

teammate
der Mannschafts-kamerad / die Mannschafts-kameradin

competitor
der Teilnehmer / die Teilnehmerin

coach
der Trainer / die Trainerin

manager
der Cheftrainer / die Cheftrainerin

match
das Spiel

points
die Punkte *mpl*

to coach
trainieren

to compete
teilnehmen

to score
Punkte erzielen

to win
gewinnen

to lose
verlieren

to draw
unentschieden spielen

leisure centre
das Freizeitzentrum

medal
die Medaille

official
**der Offizielle /
die Offizielle**

podium
das Podium

referee
**der Schiedsrichter /
die Schiedsrichterin**

scoreboard
die Anzeigetafel

spectators
die Zuschauer *mpl*

sportsperson
**der Sportler /
die Sportlerin**

stadium
das Stadion

stands
die Tribüne

team
die Mannschaft

trophy
die Trophäe

YOU MIGHT SAY...

I'd like to join the gym.
Ich würde gerne Mitglied des Fitnessstudios werden.

I'd like to book a class.
Ich möchte mich für einen Kurs einschreiben.

What are the facilities like?
Wie sind die Einrichtungen?

What classes can you do here?
Welche Kurse unterrichten Sie hier?

YOU MIGHT HEAR...

Would you like to book an induction?
Wollen Sie eine Einführung buchen?

What time would you like to book for?
Für wie viel Uhr wollen Sie buchen?

Are you a member?
Sind Sie Mitglied?

VOCABULARY

gym
das Fitnessstudio

gym instructor
der Fitnesstrainer / die Fitnesstrainerin

gym membership
die Mitgliedschaft im Fitnessstudio

personal trainer
der Personal Trainer

exercise class
der Fitnesskurs

Pilates
das Pilates

yoga
das Yoga

press-ups
die Liegestütze *mpl*

sit-ups
die Sit-ups *mpl*

walking
das Gehen

running
das Laufen

running club
der Laufklub

to exercise
Sport treiben

to keep fit
fit bleiben

to go for a run
laufen gehen

to go to the gym
ins Fitnessstudio gehen

YOU SHOULD KNOW...

Some gyms may expect you to continue paying for the duration of your membership even if you are unable to continue attending the gym.

changing room
der Umkleideraum

cross trainer
der Crosstrainer

dumbbell
die Hantel

exercise bike
der Heimtrainer

gym ball
der Gymnastikball

kettlebell
die Kettlebell

locker
der Spind

rowing machine
das Rudergerät

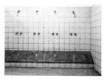

showers
der Duschraum

skipping rope
das Springseil

treadmill
das Laufband

weightlifting bench
die Hantelbank

Football is the most widely played sport in Germany. The national team have been World Cup and European winners multiple times.

YOU MIGHT SAY...

Are you going to watch the match?
Sehen Sie sich das Spiel an?

What's the score?
Wie steht es?

That was a foul!
Das war ein Foul!

YOU MIGHT HEAR...

I'm watching the match.
Ich sehe mir das Spiel an.

The score is...
Es steht...

Go on!
Na los!

VOCABULARY

defender
**der Abwehrspieler /
die Abwehrspielerin**

striker
**der Stürmer /
die Stürmerin**

substitute
**der Ersatzspieler /
die Ersatzspielerin**

kick-off
der Anstoß

half-time
die Halbzeit

full-time
**die reguläre
Spielzeit**

extra time
die Verlängerung

injury time
die Nachspielzeit

free kick
der Freistoß

header
der Kopfball

save
die Abwehr

foul
das Foul

offside
das Abseits

penalty kick
der Strafstoß

penalty box
der Strafraum

to play football
Fußball spielen

to kick
kicken

to tackle
angreifen

to pass the ball
den Ball abgeben

to score a goal
ein Tor schießen

assistant referee
**der Schiedrichter-
assistent / die Schied-
richterassistentin**

football
der Fußball

football boots
die Fußballschuhe
mpl

football match
das Fußballspiel

football pitch
das Spielfeld

football player
**der Fußballspieler /
die Fußballspielerin**

goal
das Tor

goalkeeper
**der Torwart /
die Torwartin**

goalkeeper's gloves
**die
Torwarthandschuhe**
mpl

shin pads
**die
Schienbeinschützer**
mpl

whistle
die Pfeife

yellow/red card
**die gelbe / rote
Karte**

Although far behind football in terms of number of spectators, ice hockey is still hugely popular in Germany.

VOCABULARY

blue line **die blaue Linie**	face-off **der Abschlag**	period **das Drittel**
boards **die Bande**	ice time **die Eiszeit**	power play **das Powerplay**
check **der Check**	penalty shot **das Penaltyschießen**	to play ice hockey **Eishockey spielen**

helmet cage
das Gitter

ice hockey player
**der Eishockeyspieler /
die Eishockeyspielerin**

ice hockey stick
**der
Eishockeyschläger**

mitts
die Fanghandschuhe
mpl

puck
der Puck

skates
die Schlittschuhe
mpl

Interest in basketball has grown rapidly over the last few decades, and, in fact, Germany has exported a number of players to the American NBA.

VOCABULARY

layup **der Korbleger**	to play basketball **Basketball spielen**	to dribble **dribbeln**
slam dunk **der Slam Dunk**	to catch **fangen**	to block **blockieren**
free throw **der Freiwurf**	to throw **werfen**	to mark a player **einen Spieler decken**

basket
der Korb

basketball
der Basketball

basketball court
das Basketballfeld

basketball game
das Basketball

basketball player
**der Basketballspieler /
die Basketballspielerin**

basketball shoes
die Basketballschuhe
mpl

VOCABULARY

net **das Netz**	rally **der Ballwechsel**	to play tennis **Tennis spielen**
ace **das Ass**	game, set and match **Spiel, Satz und Sieg**	to play badminton **Badminton spielen**
serve **der Aufschlag**	singles **das Einzel**	to hit **schlagen**
backhand **die Rückhand**	doubles **das Doppel**	to serve **Aufschlag haben**
forehand **die Vorhand**	top seed **der topgesetzte Spieler / die topgesetzte Spielerin**	to break someone's serve **den Break holen**
fault **der Fehler**		

BADMINTON

badminton
das Badminton

badminton racket
der Badmintonschläger

shuttlecock
der Federball

SQUASH

squash
das Squash

squash ball
der Squashball

squash racket
der Squashschläger

ball boy/girl
**der Balljunge /
das Ballmädchen**

line judge
**der Linienrichter /
die Linienrichterin**

tennis
das Tennis

tennis ball
der Tennisball

tennis court
der Tennisplatz

tennis player
**der Tennisspieler /
die Tennisspielerin**

tennis racket
der Tennisschläger

umpire
**der Schiedsrichter /
die Schiedsrichterin**

umpire's chair
der Hochstuhl

There are a whole range of water sports you can try out whilst in Germany, by the coast as well as inland. It's always advisable to seek out experienced instructors and source any appropriate safety equipment.

YOU MIGHT SAY...

I'm a keen swimmer.
Ich schwimme sehr gern.

I'm not a strong swimmer.
Ich schwimme nicht sehr gut.

Can I hire...?
Kann ich ... mieten?

YOU MIGHT HEAR...

You can hire...
Sie können ... mieten.

You must wear a lifejacket.
Sie müssen eine Schwimmweste tragen.

VOCABULARY

swimming
das Schwimmen

breaststroke
das Brustschwimmen

backstroke
das Rückenschwimmen

front crawl
das Kraulen

butterfly
der Butterfly

lane
die Spur

length
die Länge

swimming lesson
der Schwimmunterricht

swimmer
der Schwimmer / die Schwimmerin

diver
der Taucher / die Taucherin

diving
das Tauchen

angling
das Angeln

angler
der Angler / die Anglerin

surfer
der Surfer / die Surferin

to swim
schwimmen

to dive
tauchen

to surf
surfen

to paddle
paddeln

to sail
segeln

to fish
fischen

armbands
die Schwimmflügel *mpl*

diving board
das Sprungbrett

flippers
die Flossen *fpl*

goggles
die Schwimmbrille

lifeguard
**der Rettungs-
schwimmer / die
Rettungsschwimmerin**

swimming cap
die Bademütze

swimming pool
**das
Schwimmbecken**

swimming trunks
die Badehose

swimsuit
der Badeanzug

OPEN WATER

bodyboarding
das Bodyboarding

canoeing
das Kanufahren

jet ski®
der Jetski

kayaking
das Kajakfahren

kitesurfing
das Kitesurfen

lifejacket
die Schwimmweste

paddle
das Paddel

paddleboarding
das Paddleboarding

scuba diving
das Sporttauchen

snorkelling
das Schnorcheln

surfboard
das Surfbrett

surfing
das Surfen

waterskiing
das Wasserskilaufen

wetsuit
der Neoprenanzug

windsurfing
das Windsurfen

The Bavarian Alps and the Black Forest, among other locations, offer plenty of opportunities to try mountain and winter sports in Germany. There are also numerous ski resorts in Austria and Switzerland offering some fantastic skiing and climbing.

YOU MIGHT SAY...

Can I hire some skis?
Kann ich Skier mieten?

I'd like a skiing lesson, please.
Ich würde gern Skiunterricht nehmen.

I can't ski very well.
Ich fahre nicht gut Ski.

What are the snow conditions like?
Wie sehen die Schneebedingungen aus?

I've fallen.
Ich bin gestürzt.

I've hurt myself.
Ich habe mir weh getan.

Help!
Hilfe!

YOU MIGHT HEAR...

You can hire skis here.
Sie können hier Skier mieten.

You can book a skiing lesson here.
Sie können sich hier zum Skiunterricht einschreiben.

Do you have much skiing experience?
Haben Sie Erfahrung im Skifahren?

The piste is open/closed today.
Die Piste ist heute geöffnet / geschlossen.

The conditions are good/bad.
Die Bedingungen sind gut / schlecht.

There's an avalanche risk.
Es besteht Lawinengefahr.

Be careful.
Seien Sie vorsichtig.

VOCABULARY

skier
**der Skifahrer /
die Skifahrerin**

ski resort
das Skigebiet

ski lift
der Skilift

ski instructor
**der Skilehrer /
die Skilehrerin**

mountain rescue service
die Bergwacht

first-aid kit
der Verbandskasten

snow	avalanche risk	to go mountain climbing
der Schnee	**die Lawinengefahr**	**bergsteigen**
powder	to ski	to go sledging
der Pulverschnee	**skifahren**	**Schlitten fahren**
ice	to ski off-piste	to go ice skating
das Eis	**freeriden**	**Schlittschuh laufen**
avalanche	to snowboard	
die Lawine	**snowboarden**	

Whilst there are relatively few restrictions on where you can ski in the mountains, it's a good idea to have a guide accompany you if you do wish to try an off-piste route. There are also ski clinics in many resorts for those wishing to try off-piste skiing.

GENERAL

carabiner clip
der Karabiner

crampons
die Steigeisen *ntpl*

ice axe
der Eispickel

ice skates
die Schlittschuhe
mpl

rope
das Seil

sledge
der Schlitten

piste
die Piste

salopettes
die Skihose

ski boots
die Skischuhe *mpl*

ski gloves
die Skihandschuhe
mpl

ski goggles
die Skibrille

ski helmet
der Skihelm

ski jacket
die Skijacke

ski poles
die Skistöcke *mpl*

skis
die Skier *mpl*

ski suit
der Skianzug

snowboard
das Snowboard

snowboarding boots
die Snowboardschuhe
mpl

VOCABULARY

fight **der Kampf**	featherweight **das Federgewicht**	to punch **schlagen**
boxer **der Boxer /** **die Boxerin**	heavyweight **das Schwergewicht**	to kick **kicken**
fighter **der Kämpfer /** **die Kämpferin**	punch **der Punch**	to strike **zuschlagen**
wrestler **der Ringkämpfer /** **die Ringkämpferin**	knockout **der K.-o.-Schlag**	to spar **sparren**
	to box **boxen**	to fence **fechten**
opponent **der Gegner /** **die Gegnerin**	to wrestle **ringen**	to knock out **k.o. schlagen**

BOXING

boxing gloves
die Boxhandschuhe *mpl*

boxing ring
der Boxring

boxing shoes
die Boxschuhe *mpl*

headguard
der Kopfschutz

mouthguard
der Zahnschutz

punchbag
der Sandsack

fencing
das Fechten

judo
das Judo

karate
das Karate

kickboxing
das Kickboxen

kung fu
das Kung-Fu

taekwondo
das Taekwondo

wrestling
der Ringkampf

VOCABULARY

runner **der Läufer /** **die Läuferin**	final **das Finale**	starter's gun **der Startschuss**
race **das Rennen**	false start **der Fehlstart**	to do athletics **Leichtathletik** **betreiben**
marathon **der Marathon**	start line **die Startlinie**	to run **laufen**
sprint **der Sprint**	finish line **die Ziellinie**	to race **Rennen laufen**
relay **der Staffellauf**	triple jump **der Dreisprung**	to jump **springen**
lane **die Spur**	heptathlon **der Siebenkampf**	to throw **werfen**
heat **der Durchgang**	decathlon **der Zehnkampf**	

YOU SHOULD KNOW...

Germany was one of the first countries to organize women's athletics competitions, the first taking place in 1916.

athlete
der Leichtathlet /
die Leichtathletin

discus
der Diskus

high jump
der Hochsprung

hurdles
die Hürden *fpl*

javelin
der Speer

long jump
der Weitsprung

pole vault
der Stabhochsprung

running track
die Rennbahn

shot put
das Kugelstoßen

spikes
die Spikes *mpl*

starting blocks
der Startblock

stopwatch
die Stoppuhr

Golf and golfing holidays are popular in Germany, and you can find golf courses and clubs all over the country where you can hire equipment.

VOCABULARY

golfer **der Golfer /** **die Golferin**	bunker **der Sandbunker**	over/under par **über / unter Par**
caddie **der Caddie**	hole **das Loch**	to play golf **Golf spielen**
golf course **der Golfplatz**	clubhouse **das Klubhaus**	to tee off **abschlagen**
fairway **das Fairway**	hole-in-one **das Hole-in-one**	to drive/putt the ball **den Ball driven /** **putten**
green **das Grün**	birdie **das Birdie**	

golf bag
die Golftasche

golf ball
der Golfball

golf buggy
der Golf-Buggy

golf club
der Golfklub

putter
der Putter

tee
das Tee

American football
der American Football

archery
das Bogenschießen

baseball
das Baseball

climbing
das Klettern

fishing
das Fischen

gymnastics
die Gymnastik

handball
der Handball

hockey
das Hockey

horse racing
das Pferderennen

ice skating
das Schlittschuhlaufen

motorcycle racing
das Motorradrennen

motor racing
das Autorennen

netball
der Korbball

pool
das Poolbillard

rugby
das Rugby

shooting
das Schießen

showjumping
das Springen

skateboarding
**das
Skateboardfahren**

snooker
das Snooker

table tennis
das Tischtennis

track cycling
das Bahnradrennen

volleyball
der Volleyball

water polo
der Wasserball

weightlifting
das Gewichtheben

HEALTH | GESUNDHEIT

It's important to arrange appropriate cover for healthcare during your time in Germany. Healthcare for residents is funded by mandatory health insurance and provided by a system of public and private hospitals, doctors, and medical professionals. If you are a holidaymaker in Germany, ensure you have appropriate travel insurance in place.

first-aid kit
der Verbandskasten

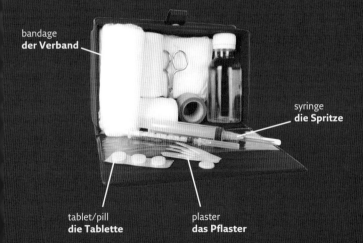

bandage
der Verband

syringe
die Spritze

tablet/pill
die Tablette

plaster
das Pflaster

YOU MIGHT SAY...

I don't feel well.
Ich fühle mich unwohl.

I'm going to be sick.
Ich muss mich übergeben.

I've hurt my...
Ich habe mir an / am ... wehgetan.

I need to see a doctor/go to hospital.
Ich muss zum Arzt gehen / ins Krankenhaus.

YOU MIGHT HEAR...

What's wrong?
Was ist Ihr Problem?

Where does it hurt?
Wo tut es Ihnen weh?

VOCABULARY

patient
**der Patient /
die Patientin**

hospital
das Krankenhaus

healthy
gesund

pain
der Schmerz

treatment
die Behandlung

to recover
sich erholen

illness
die Krankheit

health insurance
**die Krankenver-
sicherung**

to look after
sich um ... kümmern

mental health
**die psychische
Gesundheit**

social security card
**die Sozialversicher-
ungskarte**

to treat
behandeln

doctor
der Arzt / die Ärztin

pharmacist
**der Apotheker /
die Apothekerin**

pharmacy
die Apotheke

VOCABULARY

throat **der Hals**	lips **die Lippen** *fpl*	sense of taste **der Geschmack**
armpit **die Achsel**	tongue **die Zunge**	sense of touch **der Tastsinn**
genitals **die Geschlechts- organe** *ntpl*	(body) hair **die Körperbehaarung**	balance **das Gleichgewicht**
breast **die Brust**	height **die Größe**	to see **sehen**
eyelash **die Wimper**	weight **das Gewicht**	to smell **riechen**
eyebrow **die Augenbraue**	BMI **der BMI**	to hear **hören**
eyelid **das Augenlid**	sense of hearing **das Gehör**	to touch **berühren**
earlobe **das Ohrläppchen**	sense of sight **das Sehvermögen**	to taste **schmecken**
nostrils **die Nasenlöcher** *ntpl*	sense of smell **der Geruchssinn**	to lose one's balance **das Gleichgewicht verlieren**

YOU SHOULD KNOW...

In German, possessive adjectives (for example, *my, his, their*) are not often used to refer to one's body parts; reflexive verbs are used instead. For instance, "I washed my hands" translates as "Ich habe mir die Hände gewaschen".

head
der Kopf

neck
der Hals

chest
der Brustkorb

abdomen
der Unterleib

thigh
der Oberschenkel

knee
das Knie

shin
das Schienbein

face
das Gesicht

arm
der Arm

hand
die Hand

leg
das Bein

foot
der Fuß

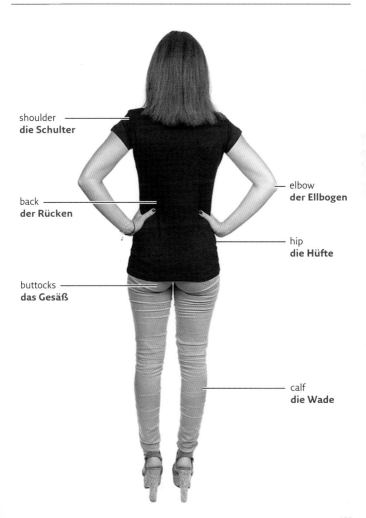

shoulder
die Schulter

elbow
der Ellbogen

back
der Rücken

hip
die Hüfte

buttocks
das Gesäß

calf
die Wade

FACE

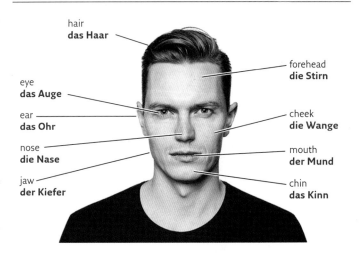

hair
das Haar

forehead
die Stirn

eye
das Auge

ear
das Ohr

cheek
die Wange

nose
die Nase

mouth
der Mund

jaw
der Kiefer

chin
das Kinn

HAND

FOOT

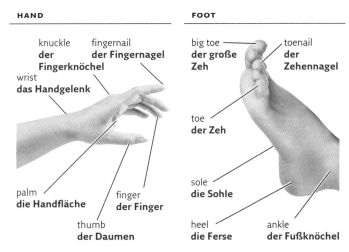

knuckle
der Fingerknöchel

fingernail
der Fingernagel

wrist
das Handgelenk

big toe
der große Zeh

toenail
der Zehennagel

toe
der Zeh

palm
die Handfläche

finger
der Finger

sole
die Sohle

thumb
der Daumen

heel
die Ferse

ankle
der Fußknöchel

Hopefully this is not vocabulary you will need very often, but it is useful to have the necessary terminology at your disposal should the need arise.

VOCABULARY

organ
das Organ

brain
das Gehirn

heart
das Herz

lung
die Lunge

liver
die Leber

stomach
der Magen

kidney
die Niere

intestines
die Därme *mpl*

digestive system
das Verdauungssystem

respiratory system
das Atmungssystem

bladder
die Blase

blood
das Blut

joint
das Gelenk

bone
der Knochen

muscle
der Muskel

tendon
die Sehne

tissue
das Gewebe

ligament
das Band

cell
die Zelle

nerve
der Nerv

artery
die Arterie

vein
die Vene

oxygen
der Sauerstoff

YOU SHOULD KNOW...

As in English, parts of the body often feature in common German expressions, for example:
"auf großem Fuß leben" meaning "to live in style" (literally: to live on a big foot)
"in den falschen Hals bekommen" meaning "to take something the wrong way" (literally: to get into the wrong throat)
"in die Hände spucken" meaning "to roll up one's sleeves" (literally: to spit into one's hands).

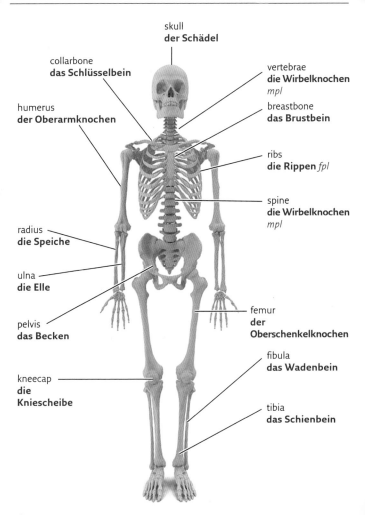

skull
der Schädel

collarbone
das Schlüsselbein

vertebrae
die Wirbelknochen
mpl

humerus
der Oberarmknochen

breastbone
das Brustbein

ribs
die Rippen *fpl*

spine
die Wirbelknochen
mpl

radius
die Speiche

ulna
die Elle

pelvis
das Becken

femur
der Oberschenkelknochen

fibula
das Wadenbein

kneecap
die Kniescheibe

tibia
das Schienbein

YOU MIGHT SAY...

Can you help me?
Können Sie mir helfen?

Can you call an ambulance?
Können Sie den Rettungsdienst rufen?

I've had an accident.
Ich hatte einen Unfall.

I've hurt my...
Ich habe mir an / am ... wehgetan.

I've broken/sprained my ankle.
Ich habe mir den Knöchel gebrochen / verstaucht.

I've burnt/cut myself.
Ich habe mich verbrannt / geschnitten.

I've hit my head.
Ich habe mir den Kopf gestoßen.

YOU MIGHT HEAR...

Do you feel faint?
Fühlen Sie sich schwach?

Do you feel sick?
Müssen Sie sich übergeben?

I'm calling an ambulance.
Ich rufe den Rettungsdienst.

YOU SHOULD KNOW...

In Germany, you need a doctor to confirm that you require an ambulance service or a patient transportation vehicle for travel to non-emergency medical appointments. Without a "Transportschein", you will be billed personally for ambulance costs.

VOCABULARY

paramedic
der Sanitäter / die Sanitäterin

accident
der Unfall

concussion
die Gehirnerschütterung

fall
der Sturz

dislocation
die Verrenkung

sprain
die Verstauchung

scar **die Narbe**	recovery position **die stabile Seitenlage**	to injure oneself **sich verletzen**
whiplash **das Schleudertrauma**	CPR **die HLW**	to fall **fallen**
swelling **die Schwellung**	to be unconscious **bewusstlos sein**	to break one's arm **sich den Arm brechen**

INJURIES

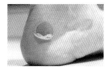

blister
die Blase

bruise
der blaue Fleck

burn
die Verbrennung

cut
die Schnittverletzung

fracture
der Bruch

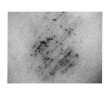

graze
die Schürfwunde

splinter
der Splitter

sting
der Stich

sunburn
der Sonnenbrand

bandage
der Verband

dressing
die Wundauflage

first-aid kit
der Verbandskasten

ice pack
der Eisbeutel

neck brace
die Halskrause

ointment
die Salbe

plaster
das Pflaster

sling
die Schlinge

tweezers
die Pinzette

YOU MIGHT SAY...

I have a cold/the flu.
**Ich habe eine Erkältung /
die Grippe.**

I have a sore stomach/rash.
**Ich habe Bauchschmerzen /
einen Hautausschlag.**

I feel faint/shivery.
Ich fühle mich schwach / fiebrig.

I feel dizzy.
Mir ist schwindlig.

I'm going to be sick.
Ich muss mich übergeben.

I'm asthmatic/diabetic.
Ich habe Asthma / Diabetes.

YOU MIGHT HEAR...

You should go to the pharmacy/
doctor.
**Sie sollten zur Apotheke /
zum Arzt gehen.**

You need to rest.
Sie müssen sich ausruhen.

Do you need anything?
Brauchen Sie etwas?

Take care of yourself.
Schonen Sie sich.

VOCABULARY

heart attack
der Herzinfarkt

stroke
der Schlaganfall

infection
die Infektion

ear infection
**die
Ohrenentzündung**

virus
das Virus

cold
die Erkältung

flu
die Grippe

chicken pox
die Windpocken *fpl*

stomach bug
**das Magen-Darm-
Problem**

food poisoning
**die Lebensmittel-
vergiftung**

vomiting
das Erbrechen

diarrhoea
der Durchfall

constipation
die Verstopfung

diabetes
der Diabetes

epilepsy
die Epilepsie

asthma
das Asthma

dizziness
die Schwindligkeit

inhaler
der Inhalator

period pain
die Regelschmerzen
mpl

to have high/low
blood pressure
**hohen / niedrigen
Blutdruck haben**

to cough
husten

to sneeze
niesen

to vomit
sich übergeben

to faint
in Ohnmacht fallen

coughing
das Husten

fainting
der Ohnmachtsanfall

fever
das Fieber

itching
der Juckreiz

nausea
die Übelkeit

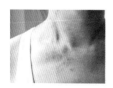

rash
der Ausschlag

runny nose
eine laufende Nase

sneezing
das Niesen

When attending a doctor's appointment, you will need to provide valid social security or insurance details, as well as ID.

YOU MIGHT SAY...

I'd like to make an appointment.
Ich möchte einen Termin vereinbaren.

I have an appointment with Dr...
Ich habe einen Termin mit Doktor...

I'm allergic to...
Ich bin allergisch gegen...

I take medication for...
Ich nehme Medikamente für...

I've been feeling unwell.
Ich fühle mich unwohl.

YOU MIGHT HEAR...

Your appointment is at...
Ihr Termin ist um ... Uhr.

The doctor will call you through.
Der Arzt wird Sie aufrufen.

What are your symptoms?
Welche Symptome haben Sie?

May I examine you?
Kann ich Sie untersuchen?

Tell me if that hurts.
Tut das weh?

Do you have any allergies?
Leiden Sie an Allergien?

Do you take any medication?
Nehmen Sie Medikamente ein?

You need to see a specialist.
Sie müssen sich an einen Spezialisten wenden.

VOCABULARY

appointment **der Termin**	examination **die Untersuchung**	antibiotics **die Antibiotika** *ntpl*
clinic **die Klinik**	test **der Test**	the pill **die Pille**

sleeping pill
die Schlaftablette

prescription
das Rezept

home visit
der Hausbesuch

vaccination
die Impfung

medication
die Medikamente
ntpl

to make an
appointment
**einen Termin
vereinbaren**

to examine
untersuchen

to be on medication
**Medikamente
einnehmen**

blood pressure monitor
**das
Blutdruckmessgerät**

examination room
**der
Untersuchungsraum**

examination table
**der
Untersuchungstisch**

GP
**der Hausarzt /
die Hausärztin**

practice nurse
**der Arzthelfer /
die Arzthelferin**

stethoscope
das Stethoskop

syringe
die Spritze

thermometer
das Thermometer

waiting room
das Wartezimmer

YOU MIGHT SAY...

Can I book an emergency appointment?
Könnte ich einen Nottermin haben?

I have toothache/an abscess.
Ich habe Zahnschmerzen / einen Abszess.

My filling has come out.
Meine Füllung ist herausgefallen.

I've broken my tooth.
Ich habe mir einen Zahn gebrochen.

My dentures are broken.
Mein Zahnersatz ist kaputt.

YOU MIGHT HEAR...

Unfortunately, we don't have any emergency appointments available.
Wir haben leider keinen verfügbaren Nottermin mehr.

You need a new filling.
Sie brauchen eine neue Füllung.

Your tooth needs to be taken out.
Dieser Zahn muss gezogen werden.

VOCABULARY

molar **der Backenzahn**	filling **die Füllung**	abscess **der Abszess**
incisor **der Schneidezahn**	crown **die Krone**	extraction **das Zahnziehen**
canine **der Eckzahn**	root canal treatment **die Wurzelbehandlung**	to brush one's teeth **sich die Zähne putzen**
wisdom teeth **die Weisheitszähne** *mpl*	toothache **die Zahnschmerzen** *mpl*	to floss **mit Zahnseide reinigen**

braces
die Zahnspange

dental floss
die Zahnseide

dental nurse
**der Zahnarzthelfer /
die Zahnarzthelferin**

dentist
**der Zahnarzt /
die Zahnärztin**

dentist's chair
der Zahnarztstuhl

dentist's drill
der Bohrer

dentures
der Zahnersatz

gums
das Zahnfleisch

mouthwash
das Mundwasser

teeth
die Zähne *mpl*

toothbrush
die Zahnbürste

toothpaste
die Zahnpasta

Eye tests in Germany are carried out by opticians or ophthalmologists; the latter will provide you with a prescription to take to an optician.

YOU MIGHT SAY...

Can I book an appointment?
Kann ich eine Termin vereinbaren?

My eyes are dry/sore.
Meine Augen sind trocken / entzündet.

Do you repair glasses?
Reparieren Sie Brillen?

YOU MIGHT HEAR...

Your appointment is at...
Ihr Termin ist um ... Uhr.

Look up/down/ahead.
Schauen Sie nach oben / nach unten / geradeaus.

Do you already wear glasses?
Tragen Sie schon eine Brille?

VOCABULARY

ophthalmologist
der Augenarzt / die Augenärztin

reading glasses
die Lesebrille

bifocals
die Bifokalbrille

hard/soft contact lenses
die harten / weichen Kontaktlinsen *fpl*

lens
die Linse

conjunctivitis
die Bindehaut-entzündung

stye
das Gerstenkorn

blurred vision
das verschwommene Sehen

short-sighted
kurzsichtig

long-sighted
weitsichtig

visually impaired
sehbehindert

blind
blind

colour-blind
farbblind

to wear glasses
eine Brille tragen

to wear contacts
Kontaktlinsen tragen

contact lenses
die Kontaktlinsen *fpl*

contact lens case
der Kontaktlinsen-behälter

eye chart
die Sehtesttafel

eye drops
die Augentropfen *mpl*

eye test
der Sehtest

frames
das Brillengestell

glasses
die Brille

glasses case
das Brillenetui

optician
**der Optiker /
die Optikerin**

There are both public and private hospitals and clinics in Germany. Some private clinics are for patients who are able to pay for themselves, so make sure your expenses will be covered by your insurance.

Which ward is he/she in?
Auf welchem Zimmer liegt er / sie?

What are the visiting hours?
Wann sind die Besuchszeiten?

He/She is in ward...
Er / Sie liegt auf Zimmer...

Visiting hours are from ... to...
Besuchszeiten sind von ... bis...

VOCABULARY

hospital
das Krankenhaus

A&E
die Notaufnahme

ambulance
der Rettungswagen

public/private hospital
**das öffentliche /
private Krankenhaus**

nurse
**der Krankenpfleger /
die
Krankenschwester**

physiotherapist
**der Physiotherapeut /
die Physiotherapeutin**

radiographer
**der Röntgen-
assistent / die
Röntgenassistentin**

surgeon
**der Chirurg /
die Chirurgin**

operation
die Operation

CT/MRI scan
**die CT- / MRT-
Untersuchung**

intensive care
die Intensivstation

diagnosis
die Diagnose

pulse
der Puls

to take his/her pulse
den Puls fühlen

to undergo surgery
operiert werden

to be admitted/
discharged
**eingeliefert /
entlassen werden**

YOU SHOULD KNOW...

The phone numbers for the emergency services in Germany are: 110 for police and 112 for fire brigade and medical emergencies. 112 is the Universal European Emergency Services number – it will connect you to the appropriate emergency service.

crutches
die Krücken *fpl*

drip
der Tropf

hospital bed
das Krankenbett

monitor
der Monitor

operating theatre
der Operationssaal

oxygen mask
die Sauerstoffmaske

plaster cast
der Gipsverband

stitches
die Fäden *mpl*

ward
das Zimmer

wheelchair
der Rollstuhl

X-ray
das Röntgenbild

Zimmer frame®
der Rollator

If you plan to have your baby in Germany, you must consult a gynaecologist who will be your principal contact during the pregnancy, as well as a midwife who will advise you on both traditional and modern ways to give birth. If you are travelling while pregnant, make sure you have appropriate travel insurance in place.

YOU MIGHT SAY...

I'm (six months) pregnant.
Ich bin (sechs Monate) schwanger.

My partner/wife is pregnant.
Meine Partnerin / Frau ist schwanger.

I'm/She's having contractions every ... minutes.
Die Wehen kommen alle ... Minuten.

My/Her waters have broken.
Die Fruchtblase ist geplatzt.

I need an epidural.
Ich brauche eine Epiduralanästhesie.

YOU MIGHT HEAR...

How far along are you?
Wie viele Monate sind Sie schwanger?

How long is it between contractions?
Wie viele Minuten sind es zwischen den Wehen?

May I examine you?
Kann ich Sie untersuchen?

Push!
Pressen!

VOCABULARY

pregnant woman
die Schwangere

newborn
das Neugeborene

foetus
der Fötus

uterus
die Gebärmutter

cervix
der Gebärmutterhals

umbilical cord
die Nabelschnur

epidural
die Epiduralanästhesie

gas and air
die Blähungen *fpl*

labour
die Wehen *fpl*

delivery
die Geburt

Caesarean section
der Kaiserschnitt

miscarriage
die Fehlgeburt

stillborn	to fall pregnant	to miscarry
tot geboren	**schwanger werden**	**eine Fehlgeburt**
		haben
due date	to be in labour	
der Geburtstermin	**in den Wehen liegen**	to breast-feed
		stillen
morning sickness	to give birth	
die Schwanger-	**ein Kind zur Welt**	
schaftsübelkeit	**bringen**	

YOU SHOULD KNOW...

A full-term pregnancy in Germany is classed as 40 weeks and 6 days, as opposed to 39 weeks and 6 days. It is also common for parents to find out the baby's sex before birth, so let your health professionals know if you'd prefer a surprise!

GENERAL

incubator
der Inkubator

labour suite
der Kreißsaal

midwife
die Hebamme

pregnancy test
der Schwangerschaftstest

sonographer
der Ultraschalldiag-nostiker /
die Ultraschalldiag-nostikerin

ultrasound
der Ultraschall

Alternative therapies are popular in Germany, but costs are not covered in the same way by all health insurance companies. It is therefore worth researching which treatments can be covered by standard insurance.

VOCABULARY

therapist **der Therapeut / die Therapeutin**	acupuncturist **der Akupunkteur / die Akupunkteurin**	mindfulness **die Achtsamkeit**
masseur **der Masseur**	reflexologist **der Reflexologe / die Reflexologin**	to relax **sich entspannen**
masseuse **die Masseurin**	remedy **das Heilmittel**	to massage **massieren**
chiropractor **der Chiropraktor / die Chiropraktorin**	reiki **Reiki**	to meditate **meditieren**

YOU SHOULD KNOW...

Homeopathy is more widely accepted by the German healthcare system than in the UK, and it is possible to find a wide range of homeopathic remedies in German pharmacies.

GENERAL

essential oil
das ätherische Öl

herbal medicine
die Pflanzenheilkunde

homeopathy
die Homöopathie

acupuncture
die Akupunktur

chiropractic
die Chiropraktik

hypnotherapy
die Hypnotherapie

massage
die Massage

meditation
die Meditation

osteopathy
die Osteopathie

reflexology
**die
Reflexzonenmassage**

thalassotherapy
die Thalassotherapie

traditional Chinese
medicine
**die traditionelle
chinesische
Medizin**

215

If you are travelling to Germany with your pet, it must be microchipped and vaccinated against rabies, and have a pet passport. Dogs must get a tapeworm treatment from a vet 12-24 hours before returning to the UK.

YOU MIGHT SAY...

My dog has been hurt/sick.
Mein Hund ist verletzt worden / hat sich übergeben.

YOU MIGHT HEAR...

What's the problem?
Was ist das Problem?

Is your pet microchipped?
Hat Ihr Tier einen Chip?

YOU SHOULD KNOW...

Most holiday properties in Germany accept pets; however be aware that dogs are not permitted in certain public areas, including some beaches.

VOCABULARY

veterinary clinic **die Tierklinik**	tick **die Zecke**	to go to the vet **zum Tierarzt gehen**
vet **der Tierarzt / die Tierärztin**	tapeworm treatment **die Bandwurm-Behandlung**	to microchip **mit einem Mikrochip versehen**
pet **das Haustier**	pet passport **der Heimtierausweis**	to spay/neuter **sterilisieren / kastrieren**
flea **der Floh**	quarantine **die Quarantäne**	to put to sleep **einschläfern**

E-collar
der Elisabeth-Kragen

flea collar
das Flohhalsband

pet carrier
die Transportbox

Germany has varied, colourful and dramatic landscapes that make it a fantastic place to explore for anyone who loves the great outdoors, as well as offering a wealth of biodiversity. There are almost 200,000 km of trails and footpaths that criss-cross the country, offering walkers a chance to discover the German countryside for themselves. Numerous nature reserves and natural marine parks can be found throughout the country.

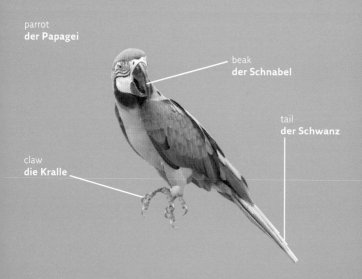

parrot
der Papagei

beak
der Schnabel

tail
der Schwanz

claw
die Kralle

YOU MIGHT SAY...

Is there a park/nature reserve nearby?
Gibt es in der Nähe einen Park / ein Naturschutzgebiet?

What is the scenery like?
Wie ist die Landschaft?

YOU MIGHT HEAR...

The scenery is beautiful/rugged.
Die Landschaft ist wunderschön / wild.

I'd recommend visiting...
Ich empfehle Ihnen ... zu besuchen.

VOCABULARY

animal das Tier	fur das Fell	wing der Flügel
species die Spezies	wool die Wolle	beak der Schnabel
mammal das Säugetier	paw die Pfote	cold-blooded kaltblütig
reptile das Reptil	hoof der Huf	warm-blooded warmblütig
amphibian die Amphibie	snout die Schnauze	to bark bellen
rodent das Nagetier	mane die Mähne	to purr schnurren
insect das Insekt	tail der Schwanz	to growl knurren
nature reserve das Naturschutzgebiet	claw die Kralle	to roar brüllen
scenery die Landschaft	horn das Horn	to chirp zwitschern
zoo der Zoo	feather die Feder	to buzz summen

Although Germany has the highest ratio of pet ownership in Europe, you should make sure that your pet is allowed to come with you to your hotel or restaurant. You can consult several websites on pet-friendly accommodation. Some public areas, like parks and beaches, may be off-limits for dogs.

YOU MIGHT SAY...

Do you have any pets?
Haben Sie Haustiere?

Is it OK to bring my pet?
Kann ich mein Haustier mitbringen?

This is my guide dog/assistance dog.
Das ist mein Blindenhund / Assistenzhund.

YOU MIGHT HEAR...

I have/don't have a pet.
Ich habe ein / kein Haustier.

I'm allergic to pet hair.
Ich bin allergisch gegen Tierhaar.

Animals are/are not allowed.
Tiere sind / sind nicht erlaubt.

VOCABULARY

fish food
das Fischfutter

cat litter
die Katzenstreu

farmer
der Bauer /
die Bäuerin

farm
der Bauernhof

barn
die Scheune

hay
das Heu

straw
das Stroh

meadow
die Wiese

herd/flock
die Herde

puppy
der Welpe

kitten
das Kätzchen

calf
das Kalb

lamb
das Lamm

foal
das Fohlen

guide dog
der Blindenhund

to have a pet
ein Haustier haben

to walk the dog
den Hund ausführen

to farm
eine Farm betreiben

budgerigar
der Wellensittich

canary
der Kanarienvogel

cat
die Katze

dog
der Hund

ferret
das Frettchen

goldfish
der Goldfisch

guinea pig
**das
Meerschweinchen**

hamster
der Hamster

parrot
der Papagei

pony
das Pony

rabbit
das Kaninchen

rat
die Ratte

bull
der Stier

chicken
das Huhn

cow
die Kuh

donkey
der Esel

duck
die Ente

goat
die Ziege

goose
die Gans

horse
das Pferd

pig
das Schwein

sheep
das Schaf

sheepdog
der Schäferhund

turkey
der Truthahn

aquarium
das Aquarium

cage
der Käfig

catflap
die Katzenklappe

collar
das Halsband

dog basket
der Hundekorb

hutch
der Kaninchenstall

kennel
die Hundehütte

lead
die Leine

litter tray
das Katzenklo

muzzle
der Maulkorb

pet food
das Tierfutter

stable
der Stall

alligator
der Alligator

crocodile
das Krokodil

frog
der Frosch

gecko
der Gecko

iguana
der Leguan

lizard
die Eidechse

newt
der Wassermolch

salamander
der Salamander

snake
die Schlange

toad
die Kröte

tortoise
die Schildkröte

turtle
**die
Wasserschildkröte**

223

badger
der Dachs

bat
die Fledermaus

boar
das Wildschwein

deer
das Reh

fox
der Fuchs

hare
der Hase

hedgehog
der Igel

mole
der Maulwurf

mouse
die Maus

otter
der Otter

squirrel
das Eichhörnchen

wolf
der Wolf

bear
der Bär

camel
das Dromedar

chimpanzee
der Schimpanse

elephant
der Elefant

giraffe
die Giraffe

gorilla
der Gorilla

hippopotamus
das Nilpferd

kangaroo
das Känguruh

lion
der Löwe

monkey
der Affe

rhinoceros
das Nashorn

tiger
der Tiger

blackbird
die Amsel

buzzard
der Bussard

crane
der Kranich

crow
der Rabe

dove
die Taube

eagle
der Adler

finch
der Fink

flamingo
der Flamingo

gull
die Möwe

heron
der Reiher

kingfisher
der Eisvogel

lark
die Lerche

ostrich
der Strauß

owl
die Eule

peacock
der Pfau

pelican
der Pelikan

penguin
der Pinguin

pigeon
die Taube

puffin
der Papageitaucher

robin
das Rotkehlchen

sparrow
der Spatz

stork
der Storch

swan
der Schwan

thrush
die Drossel

VOCABULARY

swarm **der Schwarm**	cobweb **das Spinnennetz**	to buzz **summen**
colony **die Kolonie**	insect bite **der Stich**	to sting **stechen**

ant
die Ameise

bee
die Biene

beetle
der Käfer

butterfly
der Schmetterling

caterpillar
die Raupe

centipede
der Tausendfüßler

cockroach
die Küchenschabe

cricket
die Grille

dragonfly
die Libelle

earthworm
der Regenwurm

fly
die Fliege

grasshopper
die Heuschrecke

ladybird
der Marienkäfer

mayfly
die Eintagsfliege

mosquito
die Stechmücke

moth
die Motte

slug
die Nacktschnecke

snail
die Schnecke

spider
die Spinne

wasp
die Wespe

woodlouse
die Kellerassel

coral
die Koralle

crab
die Krabbe

dolphin
der Delphin

eel
der Aal

jellyfish
die Qualle

killer whale
der Schwertwal

lobster
der Hummer

seal
der Seehund

sea urchin
der Seeigel

shark
der Hai

starfish
der Seestern

whale
der Wal

VOCABULARY

stalk **der Stiel**	grass **das Gras**	branch **der Zweig**
leaf **das Blatt**	bud **die Knospe**	trunk **der Baumstamm**
petal **das Blütenblatt**	bulb **die Blumenzwiebel**	bark **die Borke**
pollen **der Pollen**	wood **das Holz**	root **die Wurzel**

YOU SHOULD KNOW...

In Germany, white flowers are generally funeral flowers, red is for love, and yellow and orange flowers mean the joy of life.

FLOWERS

buttercup
die Butterblume

carnation
die Nelke

chrysanthemum
die Chrysantheme

daffodil
die Osterglocke

daisy
das Gänseblümchen

dandelion
der Löwenzahn

edelweiss
das Edelweiß

hyacinth
die Hyazinthe

iris
die Iris

lily
die Lilie

lily-of-the-valley
das Maiglöckchen

orchid
die Orchidee

pansy
das Stiefmütterchen

poppy
die Mohnblume

rose
die Rose

sunflower
die Sonnenblume

tulip
die Tulpe

violet
das Veilchen

chestnut
die Kastanie

cypress
die Zypresse

fir
die Tanne

fungus
der Pilz

grapevine
der Weinstock

ivy
der Efeu

moss
das Moos

oak
die Eiche

pine
die Kiefer

plane
die Platane

poplar
die Pappel

willow
die Weide

VOCABULARY

landscape die Landschaft	air die Luft	rural ländlich
soil die Erde	atmosphere die Atmosphäre	urban städtisch
mud der Schlamm	comet der Komet	polar Polar-
water das Wasser	sunrise der Sonnenaufgang	alpine alpin
estuary die Mündung	sunset der Sonnenuntergang	tropical tropisch

LAND

cave
die Höhle

desert
die Wüste

farmland
das Ackerland

forest
der Wald

glacier
der Gletscher

grassland
das Grasland

hill
der Hügel

lake
der See

marsh
der Sumpf

mountain
der Berg

pond
der Teich

river
der Fluss

rocks
das Gestein

scrub
das Buschland

stream
der Bach

valley
das Tal

volcano
der Vulkan

waterfall
der Wasserfall

cliff
die Klippe

coast
die Küste

coral reef
das Korallenriff

island
die Insel

peninsula
die Halbinsel

rock pool
der Gezeitentümpel

SKY

aurora
das Polarlicht

clouds
die Wolken *fpl*

moon
der Mond

rainbow
der Regenbogen

stars
die Sterne *mpl*

sun
die Sonne

CELEBRATIONS AND FESTIVALS |
FESTE UND FESTTAGE

"Lasst uns feiern!" Everyone loves having a reason to get together and celebrate. In Germany this usually means great food, the company of family and friends, and quite possibly a glass of champagne or Sekt. There is also a wealth of German customs and traditions associated with the various holidays and festivals throughout the year.

costume
das Kostüm

feather
die Feder

mask
die Maske

YOU MIGHT SAY/HEAR...

Congratulations! **Gratuliere!**	Best wishes. **Meine allerbesten Wünsche.**
Well done! **Bravo!**	Thank you. **Vielen Dank.**
Cheers! **Prost!**	You're very kind. **Das ist sehr nett von Ihnen.**
Happy birthday! **Herzlichen Glückwunsch zum Geburtstag!**	Cheers to you, too! **Gleichfalls!**
Happy anniversary! **Herzlichen Glückwunsch zum Hochzeitstag!**	

VOCABULARY

occasion **die Gelegenheit**	public holiday **der Feiertag**	good/bad news **gute / schlechte Nachrichten**
birthday **der Geburtstag**	religious holiday **der religiöse Feiertag**	to celebrate **feiern**
wedding **die Hochzeit**	celebration **die Feier**	to throw a party **eine Party geben**
wedding anniversary **der Hochzeitstag**	surprise party **die Überraschungsparty**	to toast something **auf etwas anstoßen**

YOU SHOULD KNOW...

In some Roman Catholic areas of Germany, a person's name day ("Namenstag") – the feast day for the saint whose name a person shares – used to be more important than their birthday ("Geburtstag"). Nowadays, however, fewer and fewer people celebrate name days.

bouquet
das Bukett

box of chocolates
die Pralinen *fpl*

bunting
die Fähnchen *ntpl*

cake
der Kuchen

champagne
der Champagner

confetti
das Konfetti

decorations
die Dekorationen *fpl*

fireworks
das Feuerwerk

gift
das Geschenk

greetings card
die Grußkarte

party
die Party

streamers
die Luftschlangen *fpl*

There are 9 official public holidays per year in Germany, and each "Land" also has its own, mostly religious, holidays. If the holiday falls on Thursday or Tuesday, many people take the Friday or Monday off as a "Brückentag" ("bridge day").

YOU MIGHT SAY/HEAR...

Is it a holiday today?
Ist heute ein Feiertag?

Happy Easter!
Frohe Ostern!

I wish you...
Ich wünsche Ihnen...

Eid Mubarak!
Fröhliches Eid Mubarak!

What are your plans for the holiday?
Was haben Sie während der Festtage vor?

April Fool!
April, April!

VOCABULARY

baptism **die Taufe**	childhood **die Kindheit**	relocation **der Umzug**
christening **die Taufe**	first day of school **der Schulanfang**	retirement **der Ruhestand**
bar mitzvah **der Bar Mitzwa**	graduation **die Abschlussfeier**	funeral **die Beerdigung**
bat mitzvah **die Bat Mitzwa**	engagement **die Verlobung**	Mother's Day **der Muttertag**
baby shower **die Babyparty**	marriage **die Ehe**	Father's Day **der Vatertag**
birth **die Geburt**	divorce **die Scheidung**	April Fool's Day **der erste April**

YOU SHOULD KNOW...

The "Tag der Deutschen Einheit" is celebrated on October 3rd to mark the reunification of East and West Germany. The capitals of the "Länder" take turns to host the official celebration. Since 1997, the "Day of the Open Mosque" has been celebrated on the same day.

All Saints' Day
Allerheiligen

Diwali
Diwali

Easter
Ostern

Eid al-Fitr
der Eid al-Fitr

Halloween
Halloween

Hanukkah
Chanukka

Martinmas
der Martinstag

May Day
der Maifeiertag

Ramadan
der Ramadan

Rose Monday
der Rosenmontag

Thanksgiving
das Erntedankfest

Valentine's Day
der Valentinstag

CHRISTMAS AND NEW YEAR
WEIHNACHTEN UND NEUJAHR

Christmas is usually celebrated from December 24th to 26th in Germany – with the unwrapping of Christmas presents often taking place on Christmas Eve and the family Christmas dinner either just after midnight mass on Christmas Eve or on the 25th. The 26th is usually spent visiting or hosting friends. The "Adventskranz", a wreath of pine twigs, is a common feature on German doors during the period before Christmas.

YOU MIGHT SAY/HEAR...

Merry Christmas!
Fröhliche Weihnachten!

Happy New Year!
Ein gutes neues Jahr!

VOCABULARY

Christmas Eve
der Heiligabend

Christmas dinner
das Weihnachtsessen

present
das Geschenk

Christmas Day
der erste Weihnachtstag

bauble
die Weihnachtskugel

New Year's Day
der Neujahrstag

tinsel
das Lametta

New Year's card
die Neujahrskarte

Christmas card
die Weihnachtskarte

YOU SHOULD KNOW...

You shouldn't wish people a Happy New Year before January 1st in Germany, but you do wish them "Guten Rutsch!", which means "Have a good slide".

Christmas lights
die Weihnachts-beleuchtung

Christmas market
der Weihnachtsmarkt

Christmas tree
der Weihnachtsbaum

Father Christmas/
Santa Claus
**der Weihnachtsmann /
Sankt Nikolaus**

gingerbread biscuits
die Lebkuchen *mpl*

mulled wine
der Glühwein

Nativity play
das Krippenspiel

Nativity scene
die Weihnachtskrippe

New Year's Eve
das Silvester

Saint Nicholas and
Knecht Ruprecht
**Sankt Nikolaus und
Knecht Ruprecht**

stollen
der Stollen

wreath
der Kranz

Carnivals – "Karneval" in the North, "Fasching" or "Fastnacht" in the South – have been celebrated since the Middle Ages. The most high-profile carnivals are held in Cologne, Mainz, and Düsseldorf.

VOCABULARY

face paint **die Kinderschminke**	headdress **der Kopfschmuck**	Shrove Tuesday **der Fastnachtsdienstag**
mask **die Maske**	Lent **die Fastenzeit**	Ash Wednesday **der Aschermittwoch**

YOU SHOULD KNOW...

Carnival traditionally precedes the fasting period before Easter, and so people used to make the most of the opportunity to eat plenty during the days of celebration, with each region boasting its own delicious specialities.

carnival float
der Karnevalswagen

costume
das Kostüm

effigy
die Strohpuppe

funfair
der Jahrmarkt

parade
der Karnevalsumzug

street performer
**der Straßenkünstler /
die Straßenkünstlerin**

ENGLISH

GERMAN

PHOTO CREDITS

Shutterstock: p19 timetable (Brendan Howard), p22 exterior below (JazzBoo), p31 minibus (Iakov Filimonov), p37 light railway (Bikeworldtravel), p37 porter (TonyV3112), p38 ticket machine (Balakate), p38 ticket office (Michael715), p38 tram (smereka), p38 validation machine (franticoo), p99 confectionery (Bitkiz), p102 cosmetics (mandritoiu), p102 food and drink (1000 Words), p102 footwear (Toshio Chan), p102 kitchenware (NikomMaelao Production), p102 toys (Zety Akhzar), p111 electrical retailer (BestPhotoPlus), p111 estate agency (Barry Barnes), p112 pet shop (BestPhotoPlus), p112 shopping mall (Radu Bercan), p136 bureau de change (Lloyd Carr), p138 postbox (Alexandros Michailidis), p139 church (Ilya Images), p139 conference centre (lou armor), p145 sightseeing bus (Roman Sigaev), p147 carnival (Tory studio), p147 casino (Benny Marty), p147 comedy show (stock_photo_world), p148 musical (Igor Bulgarin), p148 opera (criben), p155 promenade (Oscar Johns), p160 choir (Marco Saroldi), p160 orchestra (Ferenc Szelepcsenyi), p173 football pitch (Christian Bertrand), p175 basketball shoes (Milos Vucicevic), p177 line judge (Leonard Zhukovsky), p177 umpire (Stuart Slavicky), p189 handball (Dziurek), p190 motor racing (Cristiano barni), p190 table tennis (Stefan Holm), p190 velodrome (Pavel L Photo and Video), p190 water polo (katacarix), p213 labour suite (ChameleonsEye), p241 May Day (Jesus Fernandez), p241 Rose Monday (Michael von Aichberger), p243 Saint Nicholas and Knecht (Natalia Ruedisueli), p244 costume (Melodia plus photos), p244 parade (Capricorn Studio), p244 street performer (Kizel Cotiw-an). All other images from Shutterstock.